SEOUL FOOD
KOREAN COOKBOOK

seoul food
korean food
cookbook

Korean Cooking *from* Kimchi *and* Bibimbap
to Fried Chicken *and* Bingsoo

NAOMI IMATOME-YUN

ROCKRIDGE
PRESS

For general information on our other products and services or to obtain technical support, please contact our Customer Care Department within the U.S. at (866) 744-2665, or outside the U.S. at (510) 253-0500.

Rockridge Press publishes its books in a variety of electronic and print formats. Some content that appears in print may not be available in electronic books, and vice versa.

TRADEMARKS: Rockridge Press and the Rockridge Press logo are trademarks or registered trademarks of Callisto Media Inc. and/or its affiliates, in the United States and other countries, and may not be used without written permission. All other trademarks are the property of their respective owners. Rockridge Press is not associated with any product or vendor mentioned in this book.

Front cover photography © Offset/Joann Pai; Back cover photography © Stocksy/Alita Ong, Stockfood/Rua Castilho, istockphoto/4kodiak; Interior photography © Offset/Joann Pai, cover and p.212; Stocksy/Alita Ong, p.2; Stocksy/Alita Ong, p.6; Getty/Andrew Rowat, p.14; Stock Food/Joerg Lehmann, p.28; Stockfood/Brian Yarvin, p.41; Stocksy/Alita Ong, p.42; Stock Food/StockFood / Castilho, Rua, p.68; Stocksy/ Alita Ong, p.110; Stock Food/Rika Manabe Photography, p.132; Stockfood/Richard Jung Photography, p.146; Stock Food/Hein van Tonder, p.164; Stocksy/J.R. Photography, p.182; Stock Food/Rua Castilho, p.196

ISBN: Print 978-1-62315-651-0
eBook 978-1-62315-652-7

I dedicate this book to immigrant
and refugee mothers everywhere,
including and especially my own
mother and grandmother.

CONTENTS

SEVEN Soups and Stews 111

EIGHT Rice and Noodles 133

INTRODUCTION

I grew up helping my grandmother make and bury kimchi every year to ferment in our suburban American backyard. My father had dug a large pit in our shed for her to do this, and the clay pots of kimchi processed comfortably next to the lawn mowers and shovels. Like most Korean Americans, my favorite Korean restaurant was my mom's or grandma's kitchen, and rice is something I'd never give up. I spent a lot of time watching and helping my parents and my grandmother when they cooked. Since my parents both worked, I did a lot of cooking for myself growing up, tinkering around in the kitchen to figure things out when I was hungry.

It wasn't until I was in my thirties that I started to write down some of my favorite Korean recipes. Professionally, I had been writing restaurant reviews for many years, had been a copy editor for a food magazine, and had developed recipes for various clients. But I had never had the opportunity to create any original Korean recipes, so when I was hired to work as the Korean food expert for the general information website About.com, I jumped at the chance. At first, I was creating easy-to-follow recipes for a mostly Korean American audience, and I had a

blast. Many Korean Americans don't do much cooking when they are young, and so they have some difficulty recreating their family recipes as adults. And many Korean moms don't write down their recipes, so even a call to mom isn't always helpful. A "pinch of this and a splash of that" is not easy for novice cooks to translate successfully. I've been thoroughly enjoying testing different recipe variations, breaking them down step-by-step, and publishing recipes that are both tasty and easy to make.

The best part of the job, which to this day still gives me joy and goose bumps, is reading e-mails from people who tell me they've made one of my recipes and it reminded them of their mother, grandmother, or beloved aunt. Their loved ones may have passed on, but by cooking and eating their signature dishes, it was as though these missing family members were sitting and eating with them in their modern-day kitchens. I consider that a great honor.

In the past decade, my audience has changed dramatically. Korean food has become widely popular in America and around the world, and non-Koreans often write to me with questions about ingredients, substitutions, and allergies. I love e-mailing with these Korean food fans. I also get a kick out of corresponding with people who have lived in Korea for a while and need help recreating their favorite Korean restaurant foods once they've returned to their home countries. Korean food has become so on-trend that my first cookbook, *Cooking with Gochujang: Asia's Original Hot Sauce*, was published by a non-Korean culinary press in Vermont.

I wrote this book with the Korean food lover in mind, and made all the recipes as easy, but as authentic, as possible. In this cookbook, I offer you what I consider to be the best of the best: traditional Korean favorites, modern Korean recipes, Seoul-style fusion, some Korean American mom-style dishes, and some contemporary dishes with a global spin.

Korean cuisine is fun and packed with flavor. I encourage you to be creative and try different variations for any of

> "Like most Korean Americans, my favorite Korean restaurant was my mom's or grandma's kitchen, and rice is something I'd never give up."

these recipes. You'll see my variation tips throughout the book, which discuss ways to personalize classic recipes. The recipes are included with both Korean recipe titles and American recipe titles; where the recipe is a hybrid and has no official Korean title, I have omitted those. I have given the recipes labels for vegan-friendly, vegetarian-friendly, and gluten-free, and I provide easy tips for converting the recipes to your dietary needs. For guidance on spiciness, look for the chili peppers at the top of each recipe, which indicate whether a dish is mild (🌶), medium (🌶🌶), or hot (🌶🌶🌶).

Naomi Imatome-Yun
Santa Monica, California

part one

THE ART
AND SEOUL
OF KOREAN CUISINE

Chapter One

KOREAN FOOD CULTURE

Korean food to many in America means grilled meat, or Korean barbecue. The amazing feature of Korean cuisine, however, is its variety. Koreans eat a dizzying range of grains, beans, legumes, fruits, wild and foraged vegetables and roots, and every type of meat and seafood. Koreans use just about every method of food preparation: braising, grilling, drying, stewing, frying, parboiling, smoking, infusing, fermenting, and serving foods raw. And Korean dishes are served at varying temperatures, from ice cold to room temperature to bubbling hot.

Korean cuisine is often praised for its boldness and layered flavors, but it can also be restrained, refined, playful, soothing, and refreshing. Just like the bustling city of Seoul, modern Korean cooking is a mix of the very traditional and the very modern and international. In this book, I've included some of the most beloved dishes that showcase the diversity of Korean spices and preparations, from icy cold noodles to piping hot long-simmered braises. Through these recipes, you'll discover the balance and layers of flavors that you'd find on the most carefully created Korean menu.

> ### NORTH KOREAN CUISINE
> The most famous foods from the northern part of the Korean peninsula are cold buckwheat noodles (*naengmyun*), blood sausage (*soondae*), and mung bean pancake (*bindaetuk*). Generally, the food from the northern part of Korea is milder than that of the south. Because many people fled from the north to the south during the war, traditional North Korean foods are also very popular and widely eaten these days in South Korea.

FROM HANSIK TO HALLYU

Food permeates every aspect of Korean culture. *Hansik*, which means Korean cuisine, is more than just sustenance to Koreans; food is family, community, culture, and medicine. The idea of food as medicine is still strong in Korea, where traditional herbal medicine is still practiced. The "you are what you eat" philosophy has a big impact on what Koreans eat, what they value, and how food companies market their products.

Most Westerners, when they think of Korean food, think of grilled short ribs or spicy fried chicken, but rice, not meat, is the centerpiece of the Korean meal. The Korean word for rice (*bap*) is actually also used as the word for "meal." Rice is not only the staple of the Korean diet; it's also used to make rice cakes, desserts, porridge, vinegar, and alcohol. On some occasions, noodles will replace rice, but most often, a bowl of rice accompanies each person's meal. Each person at the table is also usually served their own bowl of soup or stew. All other dishes are served family style, including small side dishes, meat or seafood dishes, and kimchi. Sometimes, a large stew is served family style and replaces any other main dishes.

A Korean meal is immediately recognizable as unique from the cuisines of other countries because of the many side dishes (*banchan*) served. Korean dishes are all served at the same time and there are usually no separate courses, so the dazzling number of dishes on the table will usually surprise non-Koreans. Over thousands of years, Koreans have perfected the art of preserving food to last through the harsh winters, so many of the side dishes are pickled, salted, or fermented, and many of them are spicy. The most essential banchan is *kimchi*, Korea's unique fermented, usually spicy, vegetable side dish, which comes in hundreds of varieties. Other side dishes—there may be just one or two more or perhaps as many as twenty—can be anything from fresh vegetables to meat to seafood prepared in any number of ways.

The most common seasonings used in Korean cooking are sesame oil, fermented chile paste (*gochujang*), chile powder (*gochugaru*), fermented soybean paste (*daenjang*), soy sauce, garlic, ginger, and different kinds of onions. As a result, many of the dishes are savory and intensely flavored. Rice, milder dishes, and soups provide a soothing balance.

Because the Korean peninsula is surrounded by ocean, seafood has traditionally been a big part of Korean cuisine. Even the poorest people living near the ocean could eat clams, sea vegetables, oysters, fish, abalone, squid, and other creatures from the sea. In Korea, seafood is eaten raw, grilled, dried, stewed, and boiled. Meat, too, has always been part of the Korean diet, but it wasn't until the middle of the twentieth century that it became an everyday food. Before then, beef, pork, and chicken were generally reserved for special occasions or were luxuries available to the very rich.

Although Korea got its nickname as the "hermit kingdom" from being famously insular and resistant to outside culture, Korean cuisine has been influenced by its proximity to neighboring China and Japan. Two staples of the Korean diet, rice and cabbage, were originally introduced from China thousands of years ago. The Japanese occupation of Korea (1910 to 1945) brought traditional Japanese dishes, cooking techniques, and the evolution of Korean *kimbap* (rice rolls that look like sushi rolls or *futomaki*). European traders also influenced Korean cuisine; one of the most defining aspects of Korean food—its spiciness—is imported. Portuguese traders brought chile peppers to the Asian continent, and it didn't take long for them to become popular all over Asia.

Today's global economy has made Western dishes like pizza, pasta, hamburgers, and baked goods hugely popular in Korea, but they have been Koreanized to suit the Eastern palate. Seoul, the hub of Korean culture, knows how to take a trend and run with it, and many modern food crazes originated there, including the Pinkberry/Red Mango style of frozen yogurt and the supremely spicy and saucy Korean fried chicken (*dakgangjeong*, page 192).

Some things do not change, though, and for Korean people, the preparation and eating of food has historically been a communal event. For Koreans, sitting down and enjoying a meal with family and friends is still of supreme importance in nurturing communal life.

AUTHENTIC FUSION FOOD

During the near-starvation years of the Korean War (1950 to 1953) and the postwar period, some new ingredients were introduced to the Korean peninsula by means of US Army bases. *Budae chigae*

FROM THE SEOUL FOODIE

Daniel Gray, founder and managing editor of Seoul Eats
www.seouleats.com

How has living in South Korea affected your appreciation of Korean food?

I love the freshness and variety of Korean food, but living in Korea has helped me appreciate how healthy it is, too. Koreans take their health very seriously ("well-being" food is huge here), and they believe the perfect food ratio for a meal should be 7 to 3, or 7 parts vegetables and grains to 3 parts meat and proteins. This is why bibimbap is considered one of the nation's most representative dishes.

I also love the fearless quality in how food is served. Soups come out of the kitchen still bubbling in earthenware bowls, and barbecue restaurants put white-hot coals in the center of their tables. The Korean table showcases the characteristics of the nation—it's diverse, generous, passionate, and exciting.

How has Korea's food scene changed in the last decade, and where do you see it going in the future?

Sadly, in the ten years I've been living in Korea, the food scene has become much more westernized. Many Koreans now favor foreign cuisines such as Italian, Indian, and American food, and the "fast casual food" movement here is attracting diners who prioritize price and convenience over health.

On the bright side, there is a growing local foods and organic foods movement, too. South Korea's government has been trying to reduce the high use of pesticides and chemicals in Korean agriculture, and the rise of celebrity chefs and popular cooking shows has made organic, local food popular, too.

Daniel Gray is a Korean American adoptee who returned to Korea in 2005 to rediscover his roots. He is currently the director of iFood Korea, a startup focused on Korean food and hospitality, and his work has been featured in Serious Eats, The New York Times, Anthony Bourdain: Parts Unknown, *and more.*

is a popular stew originating during this period, when Koreans used leftover meat rations discarded or handed out by the US military (*budae* means "military base" and *chigae* or *jjigae* means "stew" in Korean). There is not an original recipe for the dish but hundreds of variations. It's mostly a lip-smacking mixture of Western meat like SPAM or hot dogs with ramen noodles, vegetables, spices, and sometimes canned baked beans.

The American army bases introduced SPAM, instant coffee, gum, chocolate, and powdered milk to Korean people during the war and postwar years, and these items are all still enjoyed to this day. Beautifully packaged SPAM gift sets are one of the most popular food gifts for Koreans to give and receive during the holidays, and Koreans put SPAM into fried rice and stews. SPAM is today more popular in South Korea than Coca-Cola or Kentucky Fried Chicken (KFC). Coffee is the most frequently consumed food in Korea now, just ahead of kimchi, and cafe culture is a big part of the social life of Korean city living. The chocolate industry in Korea is also booming; chocolate is given as gifts on holidays, enjoyed as a treat, and has become an expression of love and friendship.

After the Korean War and the rapid development of the Korean economy, global influences found their way into the culinary landscape in a more organic way. As Seoul become industrialized and Korea's economy flourished, American chains like McDonald's, KFC, Dunkin' Donuts, Pizza Hut, Outback, Starbucks, and TGI Fridays all captured the taste buds of the Korean people. These have been "glocalized," of course; McDonald's in

PEPERO DAY
November 11 is a popular gift-giving day called Pepero Day, named for the Korean stick-shaped snack that is coated with chocolate. Friends, couples, family members, and colleagues exchange pepero on this day. A fairly recent holiday, some say it started when two Korean school-girls exchanged pepero sticks in hopes that they'd grow tall and thin.

Korea has a popular *bulgogi* burger, Outback serves kimchi, and Pizza Hut serves sweet potato pizza. As Seoul becomes more and more multicultural, Seoul-style fusion food includes variations on Thai, Mexican, Italian, Indian, French, Greek, and other cuisines. It's now a food paradise, and the Korean food scene and food industry as a whole are constantly changing and growing.

Korean food's global popularity has increased dramatically in the past ten years, thanks in part to the work by Korean former first lady Kim Yoon-Ok, who headed the government-funded Korean Food Foundation. The foundation made it their mission to promote Korean food around the world with events. The growing popularity was also partly thanks to *hallyu*, the "Korean wave," or international interest in Korean music and movies. Although hallyu is still more of a trickle in America as opposed to the rising tide it is all over Asia, Australia, and Europe, Korean food has recently had a big impact on the American culinary scene.

In 2008, a Korean American chef named Roy Choi made a culinary impact when he started Kogi, a Korean taco truck, in Los Angeles. Not only did this start a food truck frenzy that eventually reached most other American cities, but it also popularized the Korean taco. The Kogi truck first made it with marinated grilled short ribs (*galbi*), and you can now find different versions of this dish in restaurants nationwide.

On the other side of the country and at the higher end of the culinary spectrum, Korean American chef David Chang has been serving a uniquely contemporary American menu sprinkled with Korean flavors and ingredients since 2004. Chang uses kimchi, for instance, in just about everything, including butter and bread. His Momofuku brand of restaurants and products is considered one of the most exciting and interesting in the food world. Partly because of the work of chefs David Chang and Roy Choi, you can find Korean influences in trendy restaurants in every major American city; *Business Insider* named kimchi a top food trend of 2015, The Food Network called gochujang "the best thing you never ate," and *The Kimchi Chronicles* television series was a big hit on PBS.

Korean fried chicken, super spicy and moist, was a trend that moved back and forth across the ocean. When the chain KFC got to Korea in the 1980s, it wasn't the first time that Koreans had enjoyed deep-fried chicken, but the fast-food chain definitely helped make it more popular. Glocalization happened quickly, and Korean fried chicken (confusingly, also known as KFC) quickly took on a life of its own. Twice fried and coated in a spicy, savory, sweet sauce, Korean-style chicken became a popular snack and bar food that inspired numerous restaurant chains across the country. The trend spread back to America, and Korean fried chicken chains like Bonchon and Kyo-Chon became a hit in the States.

RITUALS, ETIQUETTE, AND THE ART OF RESPECT

Politeness is very important to Koreans, and there is a lot of emphasis placed on traditional table manners. Being polite, properly groomed, and respectful during mealtimes is important for adults as well as children. Observance of this tradition has relaxed somewhat in recent years, but essential Korean table manners are still considered important and followed.

Confucianism has had a huge impact on Korean culture, and filial piety is still important today. Therefore, everyone at the table waits to eat until the oldest person picks up their chopsticks and starts eating. Also, no one leaves the table before the oldest person is finished. It's preferable for everyone at the table to try to keep pace with the oldest person, because it will make the whole dining experience easier. If an elder offers you a drink or a dish, it's polite to accept, as a gesture of good will. Enjoying the food is of the utmost importance; dinner conversation is not a requirement. In more formal settings and especially during meals with different generations, there are often periods of silence. If you are eating with

KOREAN TABLE MANNERS

SETTING THE TABLE

A typical table setting has a bowl of rice at the center. To the right of the rice, each person will also usually have a small bowl of soup or stew. Sometimes, the stew is served in a larger bowl in the center of the table for family-style sharing, and the many side dishes are placed around it. Utensils are placed to the right of the soup. Each setting has silver or stainless steel chopsticks (*jutgarak*) and a shallow round spoon with a long handle (*sutgarak*). Koreans usually eat rice with a spoon and the other dishes with chopsticks.

Korean tables are set so that all dishes are served at one time, without multiple courses. Korean table settings are classified according to the number of side dishes served. Everyday family meals might have three or four side dishes, but special occasions or parties call for a dozen or more.

TIPS FOR GUESTS

▶ If someone invites you to their home, it's customary to bring a small gift, like some fruit, chocolates, or a bottle of alcohol.

▶ Try not to cough or sneeze at the table. Do not blow your nose at the table.

▶ Don't stick your chopsticks straight up in your rice bowl, since it looks like the incense sticks that are burned at funerals.

▶ Don't pick up your soup bowl and slurp from it.

▶ Don't decline food or drink offered by an elder.

▶ Let the oldest person at the table start eating first, and don't leave the table before they finish.

▶ Before you eat, especially at someone's home, it's polite to say that you are looking forward to the meal. In Korean, people say *Jal mukesumneda* (잘 먹겠습니다, I will eat well).

▶ When you are drinking with elders, especially in a professional setting, turn your head slightly away from them as you drink. This is a sign of respect.

▶ There are a lot of shared side dishes during Korean meals. If they don't come with serving utensils, try to only touch the food you are taking with your spoon from the communal dishes.

friends or people very familiar to you, these rules can be relaxed.

Even with friends, some eating traditions are followed today. Sharing is a big part of Korean culture, and sharing a meal or food is important for fostering both personal and professional relationships. If you are eating a snack or have ordered your own dish at a restaurant, it's considered polite to offer it to the people around you, whether you are at work or with friends. An extension of this is that you don't fill your own glass, but you should look around the table and offer to pour everyone else's drink first. Korea is also a two-hand culture—it is impolite to give or receive things with one hand. If someone passes something to you, you should accept it with both hands. If you are passing a food or drink at the table, then pass it with your right hand and support your wrist with your left hand.

HOME FOR THE HOLIDAYS

The holidays that Koreans have traditionally celebrated are influenced by the changing of the seasons, agriculture, Buddhism, and Confucianism. There are many more being observed now, including Christmas and Valentine's Day, but the traditional holidays still hold the most meaning for families and communities.

Koreans mark important occasions with feasts and special foods, and the most important holiday of the year is *Chusok*. It's the harvest moon festival that is also sometimes referred to as Korean Thanksgiving because it is the traditional time to thank ancestors for the year's harvest. Chusok is a three-day celebration in autumn, and is a special time of eating and spending time with family. The most important food of this holiday is a special rice cake called *songpyun*. These half-moon-shaped rice cakes are stuffed with sesame seeds and/or chestnuts sweetened with honey. They are then steamed with pine needles for a distinctive, fresh scent.

The Lunar New Year (*sol nal*) is another important Korean holiday. In addition to honoring deceased ancestors and living elders with a formal kneeling bow ceremony called *saebae*, families and friends eat bowls of rice cake soup (*tteok guk*) to mark the day. Buddha's birthday, celebrated in May, is marked by visits to temples, whose monks give out free temple food (which is always vegetarian) and tea.

EAT, DRINK, AND BE MERRY

Seoul, the capital of Korea and the economic and cultural hub of the country, has more eateries per square mile than most major cities around the world. The culinary scene is exciting and rapidly changing, and is an incredible mix of the traditional, the classic, the quirky, and the super trendy. From street stalls (*pojangmacha*) filled with affordable street food to very expensive high-end cuisine, you can find food, drinks, meals, and snacks to fit any budget.

In an international survey conducted by the market research firm GfK (March 2015), South Koreans were found to cook the least out of the twenty-two countries polled. If you visit Seoul and other major Korean cities, it's easy to see why. Between the huge variety of restaurants, coffee shops, and bars, there are tented street stalls tucked into every available bit of sidewalk space. You can get everything from dumplings and noodles to spicy rice cakes and bacon-wrapped hot dogs at these vendors.

Koreans might not have enough time these days to spend hours in the kitchen, but they are certainly very passionate about eating. Since eating is a communal thing, most Koreans don't dine alone unless they are grabbing a quick bite from a street vendor. Koreans work long hours, but there is a real "work hard, play hard" attitude in Seoul. Drinking, dining, socializing, and partying are a big part of Seoul life, and it's even acceptable to drink a fair amount of alcohol during business meetings and meals. It's also a late-night culture; many restaurants, cafes, computer rooms (PC *bang*), spas, malls, clubs, bars, and fast-food places are open twenty-four hours or late into the night.

Because there are no rules on public drunkenness, it's much more acceptable to tip back a few in the street, and it's not unusual to see groups of inebriated people stumbling out of bars and restaurants. If you go out in Seoul, you may well end up at a karaoke room (*noraebang*) at some point during the night. Korean karaoke rooms are private, so you don't have to sing in front of strangers, but you should probably attempt a song or two for fun. You can continue eating and drinking at noraebangs, because food and drinks are also served there.

According to a recent Euromonitor study of forty-four countries around the world, Koreans drink more per week than any other nationality. Despite stereotypes, today's Korean drinks twice as much as Russians and four times as much as Americans. Until recently, the rice liquor called *soju* was the social drink of choice, but now beer, wine, and brand-name hard liquors are becoming popular. The drinking culture in Korea is unique, though, since it always goes hand in hand with eating. Alcohol is always served and enjoyed with bar food snacks or side dishes (*anju*). These dishes are often savory, like spicy fried chicken or squid, but they can also be as simple as nuts or fruit. It is a requirement to order anju with drinks at many Korean bars, clubs, and karaoke places. For more about cocktails and anju, see chapter 5 (page 69).

When Koreans in Seoul go out drinking, they don't just stay in one bar or club. They move from place to place during the night, which means their choices of anju and drinks also change. During a night out in Seoul, a group of friends might eat dinner at a restaurant with some drinks, move to a bar for some more drinks and anju, and then spend an hour or so singing karaoke (again, with drinks and snacks). Then they will probably hit up a last spot to enjoy more drinks and a light meal or stew. A night out in Seoul lasts until the wee hours.

FROM THE SEOUL FOODIE

Joe McPherson, founder and managing editor of ZenKimchi
www.zenkimchi.com

When I moved to South Korea in 2004, there were no Korean food blogs. I began ZenKimchi so that I'd have something to read—a record of what I eat and cook in Korea.

It was right around my arrival here that Korea's food culture began to experience a major shift. The 2002 World Cup had awakened Seoul, fueling South Korea's recovery from the 1997 Asian financial crisis. Wealth was returning, and the consumption of foreign goods and services skyrocketed, driven by people's desire to appear cosmopolitan. Young chefs traveled the world to learn new cuisines, and Korean food developed a mixed reputation. The government was trying to promote it abroad, but at home people viewed it as an inexpensive source of nourishment. Korean food was not respected the way more expensive foreign cuisines were.

This changed with the *makgeolli* boom in 2008. College kids in Seoul and Tokyo hooked in to this fizzy rice beer that was considered a peasant's brew. As the trend grew, makgeolli became an artisanal product and attention turned to other Korean foods. Koreans started to re-evaluate their own cuisine—its peasant roots, its royal aspirations, and its Buddhist traditions—and begin to feel renewed pride for it. The big trend as of this writing is the high-end Korean buffet, which showcases artisanal pickles and seasonal regional dishes.

In the ten-plus years I've lived in Korea, almost everything I miss from the US and Europe has become available here. Foreign cuisine remains extremely popular, so it will be interesting to see how far the renewed interest in traditional Korean food goes.

Joe McPherson runs South Korea's longest running food blog and has had his work featured in The New York Times, The Wall Street Journal, Lonely Planet, Bizarre Foods with Andrew Zimmern, *and more. His book, the* ZenKimchi Seoul Restaurant Expat Guide, *was published earlier this year.*

Chapter Two

FROM THE KITCHEN TO THE TABLE

The simplest way to describe Korean cuisine is to say that it is spicy and bold. It certainly can be. But the real defining quality of Korean food, I think, is its variety. Sit down at the table in a Korean restaurant or a Korean home and what you'll get is a wide variety of flavors, dishes, colors, and preparations. Traditionally, the Korean table was a balance of yin and yang, and the five colors that represented the elements (wood, fire, earth, metal, water). The yin and yang refer to the contrast you will get of crunchy and soft textures, hot and cold temperatures, and spicy and mild seasonings.

The five colors are green, red, yellow, white, and black, and the rainbow of colors makes sure that your meal is not only gorgeous, but also nutritious.

The idea of balancing flavors and colors is something that Korean mothers and grandmothers do by instinct—not something they necessarily think about when cooking. Many Koreans might not even recognize the need for five colors and flavors when eating, but they will certainly notice if their meal feels incomplete. What's important is balance, so some spicy kimchi and crunchy vegetables will balance the flavors and textures of a milky soup with rice. In the same way, some sour pickles and a hot steamed egg dish will balance a bowl of cold noodles.

ESSENTIAL COOKWARE AND TABLEWARE

You don't have to invest in a lot of fancy cookware or tableware to make excellent Korean food at home. If you cook at all, then you'll probably have the most essential cooking equipment, like pots, pans, cutting boards, wooden spoons, and colanders. The most important things you need for making great Korean meals are a good rice cooker and good knives.

However, there are a few products I recommend that will make your cooking and eating life easier. You can also use these to cook any other food (not just Korean dishes).

RICE COOKER

If you're going to be making and enjoying Korean food (or any Asian cuisine, for that matter), then a rice cooker is an essential tool. You will be glad you invested in one. Rice cooks quickly and accurately in a rice cooker, and the cooker will automatically turn off when the rice is done, keeping it warm until you serve it. Rice can stay warm in a rice cooker for up to two days, and in modern rice cookers, you can make porridge and soups, and you can use the rice cooker as a mini slow cooker. For information on preparing perfect rice with or without a rice cooker, see page 40.

Selecting a Rice Cooker

You don't have to spend much money for a rice cooker. But the one thing that is important to have is a "keep warm" function. If you have a little more money to spend, the new rice cookers with "fuzzy logic" are amazing. They have temperature and humidity sensors to regulate cooking time, and can cook white rice, brown rice, and porridge perfectly.

Here are some recommended brands that consistently receive top ratings and are widely available in retail stores and online.

AROMA RICE COOKER
BEST BANG FOR YOUR BUCK RICE COOKER
Aroma rice cookers are reliable, well priced, and user-friendly for both white and brown rice, and have keep warm settings. A few models are available for under $30, and they will last you for many years.

INSTANT POT
BEST MID-RANGE RICE COOKER

For about $100, you can get a very dependable pressure cooker that does a good job of making brown or white rice. This is a workhorse; you can also use it to make beans, lentils, soups, stews, rice, and porridge. If you are not planning to always have rice ready and waiting for your meals (like most Korean families do), this is a good compromise. You can use it for rice, and you can also use it as a slow cooker, steamer, and pressure cooker.

ZOJIRUSHI OR CUCKOO
BEST HIGH-END RICE COOKER

At the high end of the scale, where rice cookers can cost well over $500, there are two brands that dominate the market. Zojirushi is bigger in the States, but Cuckoo rice cookers are more popular in Korea. These cookers are pressure and induction cookers, so they deliver delicious, evenly cooked rice and have settings for white, brown, porridge, and other types of rice. They also have extended "keep warm" settings and sensors that can figure out how much rice is left in the cooker so that they can deliver the right amount of heat. They can also cook beans and meat dishes, and anything else you'd make in a pressure cooker or slow cooker.

NONSTICK STIR-FRY PAN

This is not an essential, but it makes cooking a lot neater. There is a lot of quick stir-frying in Korean cuisine, and the shape of a stir-fry pan (or nonstick wok) keeps everything neatly contained. I always make fried rice, stir-fried noodles, and sautéed vegetables in one of these pans.

SEGMENTED SERVING DISHES

Side dishes are what really define and set Korean food apart from other cuisines, so you'll need some small side dishes for serving meals. For everyday meals, I use contemporary segmented serving dishes that can hold 3 or 4 side dishes at one time. It makes cleanup a lot easier. If you'd rather not invest in these, then ramekins or small plates are just fine.

COOKING CHOPSTICKS

If you are good with chopsticks, then I suggest buying a couple of pairs of good cooking chopsticks. These are made for cooking, so they are longer than table chopsticks and are heat-resistant. They are useful for any type of stovetop cooking and grilling.

KOREAN CHOPSTICKS

Korean chopsticks are different from the more popular wooden Chinese and Japanese chopsticks. These chopsticks, called *jeotgarak* (젓가락), are made of silver or stainless steel and are flat. It was traditional for Korean royalty to have silver spoons to detect poison, but now everyone uses metal spoons.

GRILL PAN OR TABLETOP INDOOR GRILL

An outdoor grill is always useful in warmer weather, but a grill pan makes delicious Korean barbecue meals possible indoors during the colder months. If you like to grill often, then a grill pan or indoor grill will recreate a Korean restaurant experience better than a sauté pan can. You don't need a special Korean grill; a George Foreman grill works perfectly fine.

A FEW GOOD KNIVES

Having at least one good chef's knife will make cooking any dish easier. Look for one that is about 8 to 10 inches long, not too heavy, and that feels comfortable in your hand. It's very important that you feel comfortable holding a knife and using it. If you have a small hand, for example, you might not feel comfortable using a heavy or thick knife, no matter how expensive or how highly rated it is. You should also have a honing steel in your kitchen to sharpen your knives, and use it often to hone the blades, keeping them sharp.

If you're looking to add a knife to your kitchen, I suggest a santoku-style knife. It's a traditional Japanese knife, but now Western companies produce them. They are famous for their excellent cutting, chopping, and mincing abilities, so they are wonderful for the home cook. They usually have blades that are 6 to 7 inches long, which makes them shorter than most chef's knives and lighter and easier to hold. You can recognize them by the rippled pattern on the blade, which

helps thinly sliced or sticky food release more easily.

Other useful knives include a sharp paring knife, a serrated knife for cutting soft, tender items like tomatoes or bread, and a cleaver for cutting meat.

KIMCHI STORING CONTAINERS

If you've ever kept kimchi in your refrigerator, you know that its scent can take over all foods after a while. To prevent juice, milk, and other foods from taking on the smell of kimchi, most cooks in Korea have special kimchi fridges to hold their kimchi and other pickled side dishes. These fridges are colder, less humid, and equipped with different temperature-regulated compartments.

I keep my kimchi and other pickled side dishes in a small refrigerator (dorm room size) on my patio. You can also double-bag your kimchi jars and keep them in your regular refrigerator, or bag them and then put them in a large plastic tub with an airtight lid. Using an open container of charcoal and baking soda in the fridge will also keep it smelling nice and fresh in general.

STONE AND EARTHENWARE BOWLS
뚝배기 *TTUKBAEGI*
돌솥 *DOLSOT*

You can get really traditional in both cooking and presentation by using heavy earthenware bowls. These thick, tough bowls can be placed directly on the stovetop to make stews, soups, and mixed rice dishes. They retain heat for a long time, so you can cook with them and then place them on the table for serving. Since many Korean stews are served bubbling hot, these bowls are important for going directly from stove to table. They are not expensive at Korean grocery stores, and they will last a long time. The one that I use most at home was $12 at a Korean grocery, and it came with a lid. They are a little more expensive online, but are still moderately priced.

OTHER HELPFUL KITCHEN TOOLS

These are not essential and you can certainly cook without them, but a good garlic press, a steamer basket or steamer attachment for your pot, and a mandolin slicer will make Korean cooking easier and faster, too.

KOREAN PANTRY STAPLES

Although Korean cuisine is regional and seasonal, there are some ingredients that are used all the time. Soy sauce, soybean paste, chile paste, toasted sesame oil, crushed chiles, garlic, and ginger are some of the essential ingredients that you'll use in different ratios and in different ways.

Once you've stocked up on some pantry essentials, the great thing about Korean cooking is that you can easily swap vegetables and meats in recipes as you wish. Don't spend lots of time looking for bok choy if you have cabbage instead, and feel free to use tofu for beef or chicken if you don't eat meat.

You can keep the following basic items in your pantry, but I like to store almost all of these ingredients in the refrigerator. Most will keep for many months in your refrigerator and even years in the freezer.

KOREAN CHILE POWDER
고추가루 *GOCHUGARU*

You'll use gochugaru all the time when cooking Korean food, and it is an essential ingredient in kimchi. I also use it in other cuisines, in place of the usual chili powder found in American spice racks, so it's very versatile and keeps for many months in the refrigerator and for more than a year in the freezer. You can buy it in different textures, including finely ground or coarse flakes, and in different levels of spiciness. Most gochugaru varies in spiciness (even if you choose one with medium heat), so taste and adjust accordingly. For side dishes, use a fine gochugaru. For kimchi and stews, you can use one with a coarser grain. But if you are buying just one kind, purchase coarse gochugaru, and then you can grind it to a fine texture in the food processor if you need to.

KOREAN CHILE PASTE
고추장 *GOCHUJANG*

Gochujang is not a liquid hot sauce like Tabasco or Sriracha, which you pour or squeeze out of a bottle; it has a consistency similar to barbecue sauce. It's sticky, spicy, and slightly sweet, and adds a layer of depth and heat to soups, stews, marinades, and stir-fries. You can also use it in sauces, dipping sauces, and salad dressings.

FERMENTED SOYBEAN PASTE
된장 *DOENJANG*

This fermented soybean paste resembles Japanese miso to Westerners, but is darker and stinkier. It's an essential soup and stew base, and is also used in dipping sauces and marinades. Doenjang means "thick paste."

GLUTINOUS RICE POWDER
찹쌀 *CHAPSAL*

This might also be labeled "sweet rice powder," "sweet rice flour," or "glutinous rice flour" on the package. It is used as a thickening agent. It's called "glutinous" because it has a glue-like and sticky texture after you cook it, not because it has gluten in it. Chapsal is gluten-free.

SOY SAUCE 간장 *GANJANG*

One of the most important ingredients in Korean and East Asian cooking, soy sauce is actually a by-product of making doenjang (or miso). It adds a salty, savory flavor to soups, stews, stir-fries, meat and fish dishes, dips, dressings, sauces, and marinades. Korean cooking generally requires either regular soy sauce or soup soy sauce, which is saltier but lighter in color. I like the Sempio brand, but the Kikkoman at your local grocery store will work, too. In some soups, I use soup soy sauce, which is soy sauce that is a lighter in color but saltier than regular soy sauce. You can use regular soy sauce instead, when you don't have soup soy sauce, but you just have to adjust the amount used.

Korean chile paste

Fermented soybean paste

Fish sauce

TOASTED SESAME OIL
참기름 *CHAMGIREUM*

Korean toasted sesame oil has a strong aroma and a nutty flavor, and it's used to flavor and enhance different dishes. Because it has such a distinctive taste, a little goes a very long way. Don't pour with a heavy hand!

FISH SAUCE 젓갈 *JEOTGAL*

This pungent and deeply flavored sauce made from anchovies is used for making kimchi and for flavoring sauces and cooked dishes. I like Vietnamese fish sauce, but you can choose any Korean or Thai fish sauce you like.

MIRIN WINE 청주 *CHEONGJU*

Mirin, or Japanese rice wine, is a little bit thicker than regular rice wine and adds a slight sweetness to marinades and sauces. If you don't have mirin, you can use sake or another rice wine as a replacement. Mirin also might be labeled in the Korean store as "mirim."

RICE VINEGAR OR RICE WINE VINEGAR
쌀식초 *SSALSIKCHO*

This clear vinegar is widely used because it's mildly acidic and has a hint of sweetness. You can use it in sauces, marinades, and salad dressings.

TOASTED SESAME SEEDS
깨 *KKAE*

Toasted sesame seeds are used as both a flavoring ingredient and a garnish in Korean cooking. I almost always use toasted sesame seeds.

> **KOREANS LOVE CHEESE**
> After Mexico, Korea imports more American cheese than any other country. Mozzarella and American cheese slices are the most popular, and Koreans add them to everything from ramen to rice rolls (kimbap).

RICE 쌀 *SSAL*

The most common rice in Korean cuisine is short-grain rice, which is also sometimes labeled in the West as sticky rice, sushi rice, Korean rice, or Japanese rice. Koreans also use brown and multigrain rice, and regularly mix nuts and beans into their rice while steaming it.

PANTRY ESSENTIALS YOU MAY ALREADY HAVE

- All-purpose flour
- Black peppercorns
- Cornstarch
- Granulated sugar and light brown sugar
- Honey
- Olive oil
- Onions
- Peanut oil
- Potatoes
- Salt
- Vegetable oil
- White vinegar

I don't want to recommend too many brands for specific things, but I'll list some of my favorite brands so that you don't get overwhelmed when faced with fifty different types of soy sauce or gochujang.

My mom grew up during the Korean War and lean postwar years, so I learned to buy whichever brand was on sale.

SOME BRANDS I RECOMMEND

- ‣ Assi
- ‣ Chongga
- ‣ Chung Jung Won (for gochujang)
- ‣ Ottogi
- ‣ Pulmuone
- ‣ Sempio (for soy sauce)
- ‣ Sunchang

Many of these brands can also be purchased online, so check the resources section in the back of the book for more information.

COMMONLY USED KOREAN FRESH INGREDIENTS

CHILE PEPPERS
청량고추 *CHEONGRYANGGOCHU*

In my recipes, I use Korean green chile peppers unless they are not available, and in that case I use jalapeño chiles. For red chile peppers, I use Korean or Spanish chiles.

GARLIC 마늘 *MANEUL*

Koreans eat more fresh garlic than any other culture in the world, including Italians. It's used to season and enhance everything from marinades to soups and sauces. It can also be pickled in soy sauce or grilled with Korean barbecued meats.

GARLIC CHIVES 부추 *BUCHU*

These are similar to Chinese chives and have a stronger flavor than the thin-leaved chives you find in America. The greens are flat, and are used for kimchi, side dishes, and as a seasoning. If you can't find buchu, you can substitute a combination of scallions and chives.

GINGER 생강 *SAENGGANG*

Minced and grated fresh ginger is used as a flavoring in many marinades and Korean dishes. It is also sometimes sliced and used in stir-fried dishes, sweetened teas, or sweets.

GLASS NOODLES
당면 *DANGMYEON*

These noodles are made of sweet potato and become transparent after they are cooked. They are used in main dishes, soups, and stews. They might also be labeled as cellophane noodles in the store.

Other popular Korean noodles are buckwheat noodles (*memil gooksu*), udon noodles, and flat white wheat noodles (*kalgooksu*).

KOREAN RADISH 무 *MU*

Korean radish is a potato-shaped white radish with some green coloration on the stem portion of the root. You can use daikon radish if you can't find Korean mu, since it's similar in taste. Daikon is longer, thinner, and milder than Korean radish.

Garlic chives

Korean radish

Napa cabbage

Perilla leaves

Mushrooms

Glass noodles

Seaweed

Mung bean sprouts

Tofu

MUSHROOMS 버섯 *BEOSEOT*

Korean cuisine uses a variety of wild mushrooms. You can use button mushrooms in your Korean dishes, but shiitake, wood ear, oyster, and enoki mushrooms will take your dishes up a notch.

NAPA CABBAGE 배추 *BAECHU*

Napa cabbage is more oblong than round, and the leaves are long and mostly white. The most recognizable variety of kimchi is made with napa cabbage.

PERILLA LEAVES 깻잎 *KKAENNIP*

These fragrant leaves come from a plant that is part of the mint family; it is also sometimes called wild sesame. The leaves have a slightly minty flavor and a strong aroma. They are eaten as a side dish, like kimchi, and used as wrappers for grilled meat. They are similar to Japanese shiso leaves, which are also sometimes labeled perilla in English.

SCALLIONS 파 *PA*

Along with garlic, soy sauce, and sesame oil, scallions are used to flavor and garnish numerous Korean dishes. Scallions (young green onions) have a delicate, mild onion flavor, and in Korea, you can find them in a range of sizes. In America, there's not too much variety, so choose the thinner, younger scallions if you're serving them raw in salad or as a garnish.

SEAWEED 미역 *MIYUK*

Just like Koreans eat just about every creature in the sea, they also eat almost every sea vegetable. They use kelp (*dashima*) for making soup stocks; dried, seasoned laver seaweed (*gim*) for making rice rolls; and a softer seaweed called *miyuk* (similar to Japanese *wakame*) for making soup. These seaweeds can be found dried, pickled, or fresh and are available at Korean or other Asian supermarkets.

MUNG BEAN SPROUTS
숙주나물 *SUKJU NAMUL*

Mung bean sprouts are usually just labeled "bean sprouts" in America, and they have a mild flavor. You can use mung bean sprouts in place of soybean sprouts in a recipe, but just remember to increase the cooking time.

SOYBEAN SPROUTS
콩나물 *KONG NAMUL*

Soybean sprouts look similar to mung bean sprouts, but they have a much larger, crunchier yellow head. Because they are tougher than mung bean sprouts, they need to be cooked before eating. You can use mung bean sprouts in place of soybean sprouts, but just remember to reduce the cooking time.

TOFU 두부 *DUBU*

Although this is called dubu in Korea, Americans usually call it by its Japanese name, tofu. It is made by soaking and heating crushed, dried soybeans. It is eaten on its own or in soups, stews, and salads. You will generally find two different styles: soft (or silken) tofu that is used in soups and stews, and firm tofu used in stir-fries or as a main dish.

WILD VEGETABLES
야생 야채 *YASAENG YACHAE*

About 70 percent of Korea is mountainous wilderness, and Koreans are expert foragers. Wild vegetables and roots have always been a big part of Korean cuisine, including chrysanthemum leaves, fiddlehead fern fronds, dandelion greens, bellflowers, and shepherd's purse.

THE WELL-BEING TREND
Using food as medicine is part of traditional Korean culture, and "well-being" is a very popular buzzword used to imply that something is healthy. The well-being trend has been going strong in South Korea since the 1990s, and the label is slapped on everything from tea to instant noodles by brands eager to lure consumers.

HOW TO COOK PERFECT RICE

Rice is an essential part of a Korean meal. Keep your short-grain rice in a dry, dark place like your pantry or cupboard.

Two cups of uncooked rice usually makes four servings. The water-to-rice ratio generally is about: 1.1 cups of water to 1 cup of rice. But even if you buy the same brand over and over, you'll notice that crops differ. Some rice is drier and requires a little more water, and other harvests are much more sticky. You will discover this the first time you make a new pot of rice from a new batch.

To prepare rice: Rinse the rice in a pot under cool, running water while gently running your fingers through the rice. Do this three or four times until the water runs clear.

You can cook the rice in your rice cooker with the above proportions and with the press of a button. Or, you can prepare it on the stove if you don't have a rice cooker or want to create a crunchy bottom layer of rice.

HOW TO COOK RICE ON THE STOVE

1. In a medium to large pot, combine the rice and water (using the formula given above). Set the pot over high heat, cover, and heat until the water starts to bubble.

2. Cook it for 3 to 4 minutes at a strong simmer, watching the pot carefully to make sure the water doesn't boil over.

3. Reduce the heat to low and simmer, covered, for 15 minutes.

4. Reduce the heat even further, if possible, and simmer for another 5 minutes.

5. Turn off the heat and leave the pot on the burner, covered. Let sit for another 10 minutes without removing the lid.

6. Remove the lid and gently fluff the rice by mixing it with a wooden spoon.

7. Serve immediately or cover until ready to serve.

8. You can store cooked rice in the refrigerator for up to 5 days.

DOSIRAK TIME

In the olden days, Korean school children were sent to school with tin lunch-boxes (*dosirak*), filled with rice, some protein (egg, fish, meat, or tofu), and vegetables. The traditional lunchbox was a tin box, which the school children placed on top of the school room's heaters so that they'd stay warm until lunchtime. Lunchboxes are still common, even for adults, but the modern versions have separate compartments or containers for the different foods.

Koreans love picnicking and eating outdoors. Even though most Koreans now live in cities, hiking and enjoying al fresco meals are still popular pursuits. Korean rice rolls that resemble sushi rolls (kimbap) are the most popular dosirak and picnic food. They are filled with everything from meat and vegetables to tuna salad and cheese. People these days often get decorative, turning rice balls into cute faces and vegetables into flowers, but even a mother's plainly packed dosirak is an expression of care and love.

part two

THE
RECIPES

Chapter Three

BASIC STOCKS, SAUCES, AND MARINADES

Traditional Korean meals include a soup or stew, so learning how to make these easy stocks that are the bases of soups or stews will make Korean cooking a breeze. The dipping sauces are good to make in larger batches and store in your refrigerator, since you can use them for dumplings, savory pancakes, and Korean barbecue dinners. The sauces are the most basic ones you need to know how to make, but I encourage you to be creative when you're making them and adjust them to your own taste. If you don't like too much spice, then you can adjust the chile pepper powder, and feel free to tweak the amount of garlic and sugar you use in your sauces.

ANCHOVY STOCK

멸치육수 *myeolchi yuksu*

This stock is the basic one you'll use for Korean soups and stews. It's very easy to make and you can get the dried anchovies and dried kelp at any Asian grocery store. When making stock, use the larger dried anchovies; the smaller ones are used for side dishes. *Makes 9½ cups*

PREP TIME: 5 MINUTES, PLUS 2 HOURS FOR SOAKING / COOK TIME: 15 MINUTES

Gluten-Free

1 cup dried anchovies

1 small sheet of dried kelp (*dashima* on a Korean label or *kombu* on a Japanese label)

10 cups water

1. Soak the dried anchovies and kelp in cold water for 2 hours to rehydrate.

2. In a large stockpot, bring the 10 cups water to a boil over high heat. Stir in the anchovies and kelp and simmer briskly for 3 minutes. Turn off the heat.

3. Discard the anchovies and kelp. You can do this with a soup strainer or pass the stock through a sieve to remove particles.

4. Use the broth immediately, or for later use, store it in the refrigerator for up to 1 week or in the freezer for up to 2 months.

INGREDIENT TIP: Korean grocery stores sell premade anchovy stock seasonings in little pouches that look like tea bags. To make the stock, you just boil the seasoning bag in the water and then discard the bag.

BEEF STOCK

소고기육수 *sogogi yuksu*

A versatile beef-based broth, this stock can be used as
the base for soups, stews, and for enhancing the flavor of
savory meat dishes and stir-fries. *Makes 7 quarts*

PREP TIME: 5 MINUTES / COOK TIME: 2 HOURS 10 MINUTES

Gluten-Free

2 pounds beef brisket, rinsed

8 quarts water, or enough to
fill a large stockpot

1. In a large stockpot over high heat, bring
the beef and water to a boil.

2. Reduce the heat to low and simmer,
uncovered, for at least 2 hours until
fork-tender, skimming the top occasionally to remove the foam and fat.

3. Transfer the brisket to a cutting board.
You can slice it, shred it, and use it immediately or reserve it for later use.

4. Use the broth immediately, or for
later use, store it in the refrigerator for
up to 1 week or in the freezer for up to
2 months.

SUBSTITUTION TIP: I like to use brisket for
this stock recipe so that I can use the meat
in other dishes, but almost any beef cut
or beef bones will do. Simmered meaty
bones will also produce a rich bone broth,
which is also useful in Korean cooking.

SENSATIONAL SOY DIPPING SAUCE

A spicy dipping sauce for dumplings, scallion pancakes, mung bean pancakes, and even tempura, this is a recipe to save and remember. You can make a very simple version of this sauce by just using the soy sauce and vinegar in the same proportions. But try this recipe, which makes a really good dipping sauce. I do see dumpling dipping sauces in grocery stores that are not cheap, so knowing how to make this sauce yourself can be valuable. *Makes ⅔ cup*

PREP TIME: 5 MINUTES / COOK TIME: 0

Vegetarian-Friendly, Vegan-Friendly

⅓ cup soy sauce

⅓ cup rice wine vinegar

1 tablespoon toasted sesame oil

1 tablespoon gochugara

1 tablespoon thinly sliced scallions

1 teaspoon minced garlic

1. In a medium bowl, whisk together all of the ingredients.

2. Transfer to an air-tight glass container and store in the refrigerator for up to 2 weeks.

SUBSTITUTION TIP: If you don't have gochugaru, you can use Sriracha sauce or chili sauce in the mix.

SEASONED SOY SAUCE

양념간장 *yangnyeom ganjang*

This dipping sauce is a standard Korean sauce for vegetables, fish, chicken, and other meat dishes. You can also use it as a dip for dumplings and some cold noodle dishes. It is also the traditional dressing for lightly steamed tofu. *Makes ½ cup*

PREP TIME: 5 MINUTES / COOK TIME: 0

Vegetarian-Friendly, Vegan-Friendly

4 tablespoons soy sauce

1 scallion, finely chopped

1 garlic clove, minced

1 tablespoon toasted sesame oil

1 tablespoon toasted sesame seeds

½ tablespoon gochugaru

½ teaspoon freshly ground black pepper (optional)

1. In a small bowl, whisk together all of the ingredients to combine well.

2. Transfer to an airtight glass container and store in the refrigerator for up to 1 week.

SWEET AND SPICY DIPPING SAUCE

초고추장 *chogochujang*

This spicy-sweet chile sauce is primarily used for mixed rice dishes (*bibimbap* and *hwe dub bap*), but it can also be used as a vegetable dipping sauce or to make a spicy salad dressing. I like my "chojang" quite sweet, but you can reduce the amount of honey in the recipe if you like it on the spicier side. *Makes ¾ cup*

PREP TIME: 5 MINUTES / COOK TIME: 0

Vegetarian-Friendly, Vegan-Friendly

5 tablespoons gochujang

1 tablespoon sugar

2 tablespoons honey

3 tablespoons rice wine vinegar

2 teaspoons minced garlic

1 teaspoon toasted sesame oil

1. In a medium bowl, whisk all of the ingredients together until well blended.

2. If the sauce is too thick, add 1 to 2 teaspoons of warm water to thin it out.

3. Use immediately or store in an airtight glass container in the refrigerator for up to 2 weeks.

VARIATION TIP: For a more basic chojang, combine 2 tablespoons gochujang with 1 tablespoon of honey and 1 tablespoon of rice vinegar.

LETTUCE WRAP SAUCE

쌈장 *ssamjang*

Ssamjang is the delicious sauce that flavors lettuce-wrapped dishes.
If you've ever eaten Korean barbecue at a restaurant, then you've
probably wrapped your grilled meat up in red lettuce leaves with
some rice and this sauce. The spicy, sweet, earthy, and miso-like
elements add a complex, deep flavor to every bite. *Makes 2 cups*

PREP TIME: 10 MINUTES / COOK TIME: 0

Vegetarian-Friendly

¼ cup gochujang

⅓ cup daenjang

5 garlic cloves, minced

¼ small sweet onion, minced

1 green chile, like Korean or jalapeño,
    seeded and finely chopped

2 scallions, chopped

2 tablespoons rice cooking wine

1 tablespoon honey

1 tablespoon toasted sesame oil

Freshly ground black pepper

1. In a medium bowl, whisk all of the
ingredients until well combined. Season
with black pepper.

2. Depending on the type of gochujang
and daenjang you use, your ssamjang
may be too thick. If so, add a little water or
extra sesame oil to thin it out.

3. Transfer to an airtight container and
store in the refrigerator for up to 2 weeks.

VARIATION TIP: Everyone has their own
version of this condiment, and I like mine
to be spicy, sweet, and garlicky. If you prefer this sauce to be earthier and less spicy,
increase the amount of daenjang and/or
reduce the amount of gochujang you use.

Chapter Four

KIMCHI AND PICKLES

Kimchi accompanies almost every Korean meal, and there are hundreds of different kinds of these pickled foods. The most popular kimchi variety is made from napa cabbage and is spicy, but you can make kimchi out of turnips, cucumbers, and many other vegetables. There are also "white kimchis" that are not spicy, and "water kimchis" that are like refreshing cold soups. Traditionally, families made kimchi in huge batches during the late autumn to last through the winter. Today, most people make or buy their kimchi as they need it throughout the year.

NAPA CABBAGE KIMCHI

배추김치 *baechu kimchi*

This is the most common kimchi, and also the most popular side dish on the Korean table. Kimchi is almost magical in its versatility; it's so packed with flavor that it can provide essential seasonings to soups, stews, noodles, fried rice, and even tacos and sandwiches. *Serves 12*

PREP TIME: 30 MINUTES, PLUS 6 HOURS TO MARINATE AND 48 HOURS TO FERMENT / COOK TIME: 0

Vegetarian-Friendly, Vegan-Friendly

1 cup coarse sea salt

10 cups water

2 heads napa cabbage, cut into 2-inch squares

1 tablespoon finely chopped garlic

1 tablespoon chopped ginger

½ cup gochugaru

2 tablespoons sugar

5 scallions, cut into ½-inch pieces

2 tablespoons fish sauce

SUBSTITUTION TIP: To make this kimchi vegetarian or vegan, omit the fish sauce.

1. In a very large nonreactive (such as glass, ceramic, or plastic) bowl or pot, stir the salt into the water until mixed.

2. Add the cabbage to the salt water and, if necessary, weigh down with large plate so all of the leaves are completely submerged. Marinate the cabbage for 5 to 6 hours.

3. Remove the cabbage, discarding the marinating liquid, and rinse it in cold water. Squeeze out any excess liquid.

4. In a very large bowl, mix the garlic, ginger, gochugaru, sugar, scallions, and fish sauce. Add the cabbage to the bowl and toss to coat with the seasoning mixture.

5. Pack the seasoned cabbage into a large, airtight jar. Leave at least 4 to 5 inches at the top to allow for expansion during the fermentation process.

6. Let the kimchi ferment in a cool, dark place (such as a shady corner or countertop) for 2 to 3 days before serving or refrigerating.

7. Store in the refrigerator in an airtight container for up to 6 months.

CUBED RADISH KIMCHI

깍두기 *kkakdugi*

The pickling mixture for this radish kimchi is similar to that used in the more common Napa Cabbage Kimchi (page 54), but the crunchiness of the radish makes this one unique. The hands-on time to make this kimchi is not long, but you do have to wait about a day for the fermentation process to work its magic. It's definitely worth the wait; this kimchi is the one we always have trouble keeping in the house! *Serves 10 as a side dish*

PREP TIME: 30 MINUTES, PLUS 2 HOURS TO MARINATE AND 24 HOURS TO FERMENT / COOK TIME: 0

Vegetarian-Friendly, Vegan-Friendly

3½ pounds Korean radish, peeled and cut into ¾-inch cubes

2 cups sea salt, plus 1 tablespoon

5 teaspoons sugar

6 tablespoons gochugaru

½ large onion, finely chopped

2 garlic cloves, minced

1 teaspoon fish sauce

2 scallions, chopped

1-inch piece fresh ginger, peeled and finely chopped

1. Put the radish in a large bowl and cover with 2 cups salt. Mix gently to combine. Let sit at room temperature for 2 hours. Any water will drain away, collecting at the bottom of the bowl.

2. Rinse the radish well with cold water and drain thoroughly.

3. In a large bowl, combine the sugar, gochugaru, onion, garlic, fish sauce, scallions, ginger, and the remaining 1 tablespoon salt and mix well. Add the radish and toss to coat.

4. Transfer the seasoned radish into an airtight glass container (leaving 2 inches at the top), cover, and store at room temperature for at least 24 hours.

5. Serve immediately, or store in an airtight glass container in the refrigerator for up to 2 months.

SUBSTITUTION TIP: For a vegan or vegetarian kimchi, omit the fish sauce.

STUFFED CUCUMBER KIMCHI

오이소박이 *oisobagi*

I probably say this about all different types of kimchi, but this Stuffed Cucumber Kimchi (*oisobagi*) is a favorite of mine. When you make this in the summer when cucumbers are in season, its fresh, snappy texture is unbeatable. And it can be eaten the day you make it. *Serves 10 as a side dish*

PREP TIME: 30 MINUTES, PLUS 30 MINUTES TO MARINATE AND
8 TO 12 HOURS TO FERMENT / COOK TIME: 0

Vegetarian-Friendly, Vegan-Friendly

10 Korean, pickling, or kirby cucumbers, with the ends trimmed

¼ cup sea salt

4 garlic cloves, minced

½ cup gochugaru

½ cup Asian chives, cut into 1-inch pieces

⅓ cup fish sauce

⅓ cup shredded carrots

2 tablespoons sugar

1. Stand one cucumber up on its end on the cutting board and slice down the middle vertically without cutting all the way through the end. Rotate the cucumber and make another vertical cut without going through the end, so that the second cut is perpendicular to the first. Repeat for the remaining 9 cucumbers.

2. Fill a large bowl with water and add the salt. Stir to dissolve. Add the cut cucumbers in this salt bath and keep them submerged for 30 minutes. If necessary, weight them down with a plate so they remain covered with the salt bath.

3. While the cucumbers are marinating, mix the garlic, gochugaru, chives, fish sauce, carrots, and sugar together in a large bowl.

4. When the cucumbers have marinated for 30 minutes, remove them from the salt bath. Do not rinse them. Stuff the seasoning mixture into each cucumber, filling the spaces between the connected spears. Do not rinse out the large bowl that held the seasoning mixture. Lay cucumbers down next to each other in an airtight glass container.

5. Fill the seasoning bowl with 1 cup of water, stirring to mix it with the remaining seasoning in the bowl. Pour this mixture over the cucumbers in the containers until they are almost submerged.

6. Cover with a tight-fitting lid and store at room temperature for 8 to 12 hours. Serve immediately or store in the refrigerator for up to 1 month.

INGREDIENT TIP: You can find small Korean cucumbers at Asian markets. If you can't find kirby cucumbers, you can use another unwaxed, thin-skinned pickling cucumber. It's important to use thin-skinned cucumbers for pickling, not the large, thick-skinned cucumbers you commonly find at American grocery stores.

SUBSTITUTION TIP: For a vegan or vegetarian kimchi, omit the fish sauce.

VARIATION TIP: Stuffed Tomato Kimchi. When tomatoes are in season, swap out the cucumbers for tomatoes for a tasty, fresh kimchi. You don't have to salt the tomatoes before pickling. Make an additional vertical cut in the tomato so there's room for the stuffing mixture.

WHITE RADISH KIMCHI

동치미 *dongchimi*

Dongchimi is a nonspicy kimchi that is vinegary and slightly sweet. It falls into the "white" and "water" categories of the hundreds of different types of kimchi. Although dongchimi requires a few days of brining, it is simple to make and lasts for a long time in the refrigerator. Although this kimchi was traditionally made and eaten in the winter in Korea, you can make it year-round now because radishes are so widely available. With a tart, refreshing flavor, I love this white water kimchi during the summer as both a side dish and as the soup base for cold noodles. *Serves 15 as a side dish*

PREP TIME: 15 MINUTES, PLUS 24 HOURS TO SALT AND 24 HOURS TO FERMENT / COOK TIME: 0

Vegetarian-Friendly, Vegan-Friendly

8 medium Korean radishes (or 6 large daikon radishes), peeled and sliced into 1-inch pieces

6 tablespoons sea salt, divided

4 tablespoons sugar, divided

10 cups water, at room temperature

4 garlic cloves, thinly sliced

3 to 4 scallions, sliced into 2-inch pieces

Thinly sliced carrots, chiles (like jalapeño), or Asian pears (optional)

1. In a large bowl, add the radishes, 3 tablespoons of the salt, and 2 tablespoons of the sugar, and toss to coat. Let stand at room temperature for 1 day.

2. After brining, in another large bowl, combine the remaining 3 tablespoons salt and 2 tablespoons sugar with the water and stir until dissolved. Add the salted radishes, garlic, scallions, and carrots or chiles or Asian pears (if using). Let stand at room temperature for 24 hours.

3. After about 1 day, the brine will have a tart, vinegary flavor. Transfer the container to the refrigerator to chill. After chilling, the kimchi is ready to eat.

4. To serve, ladle the vegetables and a generous amount of the brine into a cup or small bowl.

5. Store in an airtight glass container in the refrigerator for up to 1 month.

SUBSTITUTION TIP: I like this kimchi to be just a little sweet, the way my grandmother made it, but I've noticed that modern dongchimi served in restaurants is very sweet. So feel free to add more sugar if that's what you prefer.

VARIATION TIP: An awesome thing to make with this water kimchi is cold dongchimi noodles. To make, cook some thin Asian wheat flour noodles (*somen*), cool them under running water, drain them, and then ladle them into a bowl of dongchimi.

PICKLING TIP: It's best to make this kimchi in a large glass jar, but whatever container you use, make sure to leave room at the top for the gases released during the fermentation process.

SCALLION KIMCHI

파김치 *pa kimchi*

This is a great kimchi recipe to make and store if you have a smaller kitchen or limited refrigerator space. A little Scallion Kimchi goes a long way, so you don't need to make lots to add flavor to your meals. *Serves 12 as a side dish*

PREP TIME: 20 MINUTES, PLUS 30 MINUTES TO MARINATE AND 24 HOURS TO FERMENT / COOK TIME: 10 MINUTES

Vegetarian-Friendly, Vegan-Friendly

2 pounds scallions, trimmed

⅓ cup fish sauce

1 cup water

2 tablespoons sweet rice flour

2 Asian pears, peeled, cored, and puréed

4 garlic cloves, puréed

1-inch piece fresh ginger, peeled and puréed

2 cups gochugaru

2 tablespoons toasted sesame seeds

1½ tablespoons sugar

1 teaspoon rice wine vinegar

INGREDIENT TIP: Sweet rice flour may be labeled "glutinous rice flour" at your local Asian, Korean, Chinese, or Indian market.

INGREDIENT TIP: Many grocery stores use the names scallions, spring onions, and green onions interchangeably, but when I recommend scallions, I am talking about the young green onions that do not have a white bulb at the root end. The white part of the scallion should be straight-sided, since it is immature and has not yet started to form a bulb.

1. Dry the scallions well with paper towels. In a large mixing bowl, add the scallions, pour the fish sauce over them, and toss to coat well. Let sit at room temperature for 20 to 30 minutes.

2. While the scallions are marinating, prepare the sauce. In a small saucepan over medium heat, combine the water and sweet rice flour, stirring gently. Heat until bubbly. Remove from the heat and let cool.

3. While the flour mixture is cooling, make a seasoning paste. In a large mixing bowl, mix together the puréed pears, garlic, and ginger. Add the gochugaru, sesame seeds, sugar, and vinegar and mix well.

4. When the flour mixture has cooled, mix it thoroughly into the bowl with the seasoning paste. Pour the seasoning mixture over the scallions and fish sauce. Mix gently and thoroughly.

5. Place the scallions into an airtight glass jar, arranging them neatly. Pour the remaining sauce over the top. Screw on the lid loosely and let sit at room temperature for 1 day and up to 2 days.

6. Store in the refrigerator for up to 1 month.

WHITE KIMCHI

백김치 *baek kimchi*

Although the most recognizable types of kimchi are spicy, this white kimchi is not. It's a refreshing side dish that brings balance to super spicy stews and soups. It is relatively easy to make if you're patient. *Makes 1 gallon*

PREP TIME: 30 MINUTES, PLUS 8 HOURS TO MARINATE AND 12 HOURS TO FERMENT / COOK TIME: 0

Vegetarian-Friendly,
Vegan-Friendly, Gluten-Free

6 tablespoons coarse kosher salt, divided

1 large head napa cabbage,
     trimmed and quartered lengthwise
     with root end left intact

1 tablespoon sugar

2 small jalapeño chiles, seeded and quartered

10 scallions, 6 cut into matchsticks
     and 4 thinly sliced

7 garlic cloves, 3 of them
     minced, 4 thinly sliced

1¼ pounds carrots, shredded

3-inch piece fresh ginger, peeled and minced

SUBSTITUTION TIP: Experiment with adding thinly sliced, brightly colored bell peppers to this kimchi for a more colorful side dish.

1. Mix 5 tablespoons of the salt with 6 cups water in a stockpot.

2. Add the cabbage, placing it cut-side up. Top with a heavy plate if necessary to keep the cabbage submerged in the salty water. Let stand at room temperature for at least 8 hours.

3. Drain the cabbage, discarding the liquid, and rinse in cold running water.

4. In a large bowl or canning jar, mix the remaining 1 tablespoon salt with the sugar and 4 cups water. Mix well to combine.

5. In a large bowl, mix together the jalapeño chiles, scallions, garlic, carrots, and ginger.

6. Stuff a small amount of this vegetable mixture between each of the cabbage leaves. Place the stuffed cabbage into the prepared brine in the bowl or jar. Top with a heavy plate to keep the cabbage submerged in the brine, and let sit at room temperature for 12 hours. Transfer to an airtight container.

7. Put in the refrigerator and, if possible, let sit for another 12 hours before serving.

8. To serve, remove the cabbage quarters from the brine and cut into 1-inch slices.

QUICK WATER KIMCHI

나박김치 *nabak kimchi*

This white kimchi is a popular summertime side dish that is
not spicy, and is refreshing and full of crispy vegetables. It
makes a perfect topping for cold noodle soups and a tasty side
for grilled meat or fish dishes. *Serves 15 as a side dish*

PREP TIME: 1 HOUR, PLUS 40 MINUTES TO SALT AND 2 DAYS TO FERMENT / COOK TIME: 0

Vegetarian-Friendly,
Vegan-Friendly, Gluten-Free

2 cups of chopped napa cabbage,
    cut into 1-inch cubes

½ cup chopped scallions

½ Asian pear, peeled and cut into cubes

½ apple, cut into cubes

¼ carrot, cut into cubes

3 garlic cloves, sliced

2 tablespoons sea salt

4 cups water

2 tablespoons sugar

1. In a large bowl, mix together the cabbage, scallions, pear, apple, carrot, and garlic. Add the salt and stir to mix well. Let the mixture sit at room temperature for 40 minutes.

2. Transfer the mixture to a extra large glass jar.

3. In a large glass measuring cup, combine the water and sugar and stir to dissolve. Pour the mixture into the jar, making sure to cover the mixture with liquid. Cover tightly and refrigerate for at least 48 hours before eating.

4. Store in the refrigerator for up to 1 month.

INGREDIENT TIP: You can omit the fruit for a simpler version, and you can also add green chiles to this kimchi for a little spice.

PICKLED PERILLA LEAVES

깻잎장아찌 *kkaennipjangajji*

This is one of my favorite summertime dishes, because we always grew perilla (or *kkaennip*) in our garden while I was growing up. Perilla leaves have a strong and fresh aroma, and the scent always reminds me of childhood summers. This side dish is also easy to make and is ready to eat in just a few hours. Kkaennip translates from the Korean as "sesame leaf," but that's actually a misnomer because the plant is not related to the sesame plant. *Serves 12 as a side dish*

PREP TIME: 30 MINUTES, PLUS 10 HOURS TO MARINATE / COOK TIME: 0

Vegetarian-Friendly, Vegan-Friendly

3 to 4 bunches of fresh Korean perilla leaves, or about 60 medium homegrown leaves

¼ cup soy sauce

¼ cup water

2 tablespoons gochugaru

2 tablespoons sweet onion, puréed or minced

2 tablespoons minced garlic

2 scallions, finely chopped

1. Wash and dry each perilla leaf thoroughly, shaking each to remove excess water.

2. Lay them in a colander lined with paper towels to dry. (If you purchased prewashed perilla leaves, you can skip this step).

3. While the perilla leaves are drying, in a large bowl, combine the soy sauce, water, gochugaru, onion, garlic, and scallions. Stir to mix well.

4. In a large glass container that has a lid, lay one perilla leaf down and spread a small amount of the sauce on the leaf with the back of a spoon. Repeat with the rest of the leaves and the sauce, piling them atop each other Make sure to lay the leaves down neatly so the stems point in the same direction. If you have any sauce leftover, pour it over the stack of leaves. If you run out of sauce, tip the perilla container slightly and spoon some of the sauce from the bottom of the stack of leaves and drizzle it over the top. ➤

PICKLED PERILLA LEAVES
continued

5. Cover the container with the lid and let sit at room temperature for about 2 hours. Transfer to the refrigerator and chill for about 8 hours.

6. Serve as a side dish with rice.

7. Store in an airtight container in the refrigerator for up to 1 month.

SERVING TIP: Using chopsticks, pick up a piece of kkaennip by the stem, place it on top of rice, and use the leaf as a wrap to scoop up some of the rice.

INGREDIENT TIP: Kkaennip is easy to grow in a home garden. In fact, it grows like a weed and is nearly impossible to kill. Its strong scent also keeps pesky bugs away.

PICKLED CUCUMBER

오이 *oi*

These Korean pickles are delicious and incredibly easy to make.
With just three ingredients, you can make a large batch to
last many meals. To serve, slice the pickles and serve plain or
slice and garnish with scallions or chives. *Serves 8 to 16*

PREP TIME: 30 MINUTES, PLUS 4 DAYS TO PICKLE / COOK TIME: 10 MINUTES

Vegetarian-Friendly,
Vegan-Friendly, Gluten-Free

20 to 50 kirby or pickling cucumbers

Coarse sea salt

White vinegar

1. Stack the cucumbers neatly in a glass container.

2. Add water to cover, then pour the water out into a measuring cup, making a note of how much water there is. Transfer the water to a large saucepan and add one-twelfth that amount of salt (so if you have 3 cups water, you would add ¼ cup salt), and stir to combine. Add 1 tablespoon of vinegar for every 20 small cucumbers, and stir to mix. Bring to a boil. Remove from the heat as soon as the water reaches a boil. Immediately pour the salted water into the glass container, covering the cucumbers.

3. Place a small dish on top of the cucumbers to weigh them down and keep them submerged in the brine. Store in a cool, dark place for 4 to 5 days.

4. Eat immediately, or transfer them to the refrigerator to store for up to 3 months.

SERVING TIP: The pickles might be too salty for your taste after brining. If so, adjust the saltiness by rinsing the pickle slices in water or serving them in a bowl of cold water.

EASY PICKLED CHILES

고추장아찌 *gochujangajji*

These pickled chiles in soy sauce and vinegar are a popular Korean side dish of which a little goes a long way. These are best made with Korean chiles, which are sweeter and less spicy than jalapeños. Because of the spiciness of the chiles and the impossibility (and inadvisability) of eating many of them in one sitting, even a small a jar of these can last you a couple of weeks. *Makes ½ pint*

PREP TIME: 5 MINUTES, PLUS 2 DAYS TO PICKLE / COOK TIME: 5 MINUTES

Vegetarian-Friendly, Vegan-Friendly

2 cups white vinegar

½ cup soy sauce

1 teaspoon superfine or extra fine sugar

1 teaspoon sea salt

5 Korean chiles, sliced crosswise into thin rounds

1. In a large bowl, whisk together the vinegar, soy sauce, sugar, and salt until the sugar and salt are dissolved, to make the brine mixture.

2. Place the chiles neatly into an airtight glass container and pour the brine mixture over them.

3. Cover and refrigerate for at least 2 days.

4. Store in the refrigerator for up to 2 months.

INGREDIENT TIP: If you can't find Korean chiles, you can make these with jalapeños, which are more widely available in the United States. Add an additional 1 teaspoon sugar to the mix to make up for the spicey level of the chiles. You can also remove most of the chile seeds so that the pickled jalapeños won't be too spicy.

QUICK PICKLES

These quick cucumber pickles go with everything, from sandwiches to a full Korean meal. With just four ingredients, you can make this really snappy, crunchy cucumber salad in 20 minutes. For thinner slices or strips, use a mandoline. For this recipe, you can use 1 long English cucumber if you don't have access to small pickling cucumbers: First cut the cucumber in half, scrape out most of the seeds, and then drain the cucumber on paper towels before slicing. *Serves 4*

PREP TIME: 10 MINUTES, PLUS 20 MINUTES TO MARINATE / COOK TIME: 0

Vegetarian-Friendly,
Vegan-Friendly, Gluten-Free

4 small Korean or kirby cucumbers, trimmed

3 tablespoons sugar

1 tablespoon sea salt

¼ cup vinegar

1. Cut the cucumbers into uniform strips or round slices.

2. Put the cucumbers in a medium bowl and sprinkle with the sugar and salt. Toss gently to coat.

3. Add the vinegar, stirring to coat the cucumber slices well.

4. Refrigerate for 20 minutes before serving.

PICKLING TIP: You can double or triple this recipe for a group or if you want it to last for a few days. These are very easy to gobble up! Store in an airtight glass container in the refrigerator for up to 1 week.

Chapter Five

APPETIZERS AND ANJU
(BAR FOOD)

Korean meals are distinct from many other cuisines because, traditionally, all the courses are usually served at the same time. However, these days there are some popular dishes that are served as appetizers in restaurants around the world. Savory appetizers are also popular as snacks, so dishes like scallion pancakes and spicy rice cakes are commonly enjoyed as casual or street food snacks.

In Korean bars and nightclubs, you don't order just cocktails, since drinking and eating go hand-in-hand. This is also true for many bars in Koreatowns around the world. *Anju* is the word for "drinking snack" in Korea, and there are no real rules for these shared dishes. They can be spicy and savory, an assortment of finger foods, or sweet and salty.

SCALLION PANCAKE

파전 *pajeon*

Pa is the Korean word for scallion and *jun*, or *jeon*, means any food that is coated in batter and pan-fried. This Korean scallion pancake recipe works as a hearty snack, an appetizer, or a side dish in a Korean meal. As with most Korean dishes, you can tweak it to your own tastes. Red chiles, onions, carrots, zucchini, mushrooms, and kimchi are all popular additions in pajeon. Serve these pancakes with Seasoned Soy Sauce (page 49) or Sweet and Spicy Dipping Sauce (page 50). *Serves 6 as a side dish*

PREP TIME: 15 MINUTES / COOK TIME: 20 MINUTES

Vegetarian-Friendly, Gluten-Free

2 cups all-purpose flour

2 eggs, beaten

1½ cups water

6 scallions, halved lengthwise and cut into 2- to 3-inch lengths

1 teaspoon salt

Vegetable oil for cooking

INGREDIENT TIP: You can also make these pancakes using readymade "Korean Pancake Batter" (*buchimgae*) from a Korean or Asian grocery store. Add ¾ cup water for every 1 cup of dry mix and add whatever vegetables you wish.

1. In a medium bowl, mix together all of the ingredients except for the vegetable oil, and let sit for about 10 minutes. Check the consistency before cooking. The batter should be a little bit runnier than American pancake batter, so the pajeon cooks quickly and evenly.

2. Heat a medium skillet over medium heat and coat with a thin layer of vegetable oil.

3. Pour the batter into the skillet, coating the bottom of the pan in a thin layer (about one-third of the batter should fill a medium skillet).

4. Cook for 3 to 4 minutes, until the batter is set and golden brown on the bottom. Turn over the pancake with help of a spatula or plate (or flip it in the air if you are good at that) and finish by cooking 1 to 2 more minutes, adding more oil if necessary. Transfer the pancake to a warm plate. Repeat, to cook the remaining pancakes.

5. Before serving, cut into triangles (like a pizza). Serve with seasoned soy sauce or spicy dipping sauce.

KIMCHI AND BACON PANCAKE

김치전 *kimchijeon*

This kimchi pancake recipe is a great way to use leftover kimchi and is easy to make. *Kimchijeon* works as a hearty snack, an appetizer, or a side dish in a Korean meal. As with most Korean recipes and dishes, you can tweak it to your own taste with the addition of other vegetables, meat, or seafood. Serve these pancakes with Seasoned Soy Sauce (page 49) or Sweet and Spicy Dipping Sauce (page 50). *Serves 6 as a side dish*

PREP TIME: 15 MINUTES / COOK TIME: 20 MINUTES

Vegetarian-Friendly, Gluten-Free

2 cups all-purpose flour

2 eggs, beaten

1½ cups water

1 to 2 cups chopped Napa Cabbage Kimchi (page 54)

3 pieces bacon, cooked, drained, and cut into strips

½ onion, finely chopped

1 teaspoon salt

Vegetable oil for cooking

INGREDIENT TIP: As with the recipe for scallion pancakes on the previous page, you can also make these using readymade "Korean Pancake Batter" (*buchimgae*) from a Korean or Asian grocery store. Add ¾ cup water for every 1 cup of dry mix and add whatever vegetables you wish.

1. In a medium bowl, mix together all of the ingredients except for the vegetable oil, and let sit for about 10 minutes. Check the consistency before cooking. The batter should be a little bit runnier than American pancake batter, so that it cooks quickly and evenly.

2. Heat a medium skillet over medium heat and coat with a thin layer of vegetable oil.

3. Pour the batter into the skillet, coating the bottom of the pan in a thin layer (about one-third of the batter should fill a medium skillet). Cook for 3 to 4 minutes, until the batter is set and golden brown on the bottom. Turn over the pancake with the help of a spatula or plate (or flip it in the air if you are good at that) and finish by cooking 1 to 2 more minutes, adding more oil if necessary. Transfer the pancake to a warmed plate. Repeat, to cook the remaining pancakes.

4. To serve, you can cut in half or in quarters if you wish. Serve with seasoned soy sauce or spicy dipping sauce.

MUNG BEAN PANCAKE

빈대떡 *bindaetteok*

These savory pancakes are made with ground mung beans, chopped kimchi, bean sprouts, and pork, and they are full of protein and good flavor. They are quite hearty, so while they can be a snack or side dish, they can also serve as the main dish to your lunch or dinner. Since the batter is made with beans, this is a good dish for gluten-free folks (use gluten-free soy sauce) or people trying to up their protein intake. *Serves 6 as a side dish*

PREP TIME: 15 MINUTES / COOK TIME: 20 MINUTES

Vegetarian-Friendly, Gluten-Free

2 cups dried, peeled mung beans, soaked overnight and drained

4 ounces boneless pork loin, trimmed and finely chopped

½ cup kimchi, rinsed, strained, and finely chopped, plus ½ cup of the kimchi pickling liquid

1½ cups mung bean sprouts, chopped

1 tablespoon salt

6 scallions, halved lengthwise and cut into 1-inch pieces

5 garlic cloves, finely chopped

Vegetable oil for cooking

¼ cup soy sauce (or gluten-free soy sauce)

1 tablespoon white vinegar

1. In a food processor, purée the mung beans with 1¾ cups water until smooth.

2. Transfer to a large bowl and add the pork, kimchi and kimchi pickling liquid, sprouts, salt, scallions, and garlic. Stir to mix well.

3. Heat 2 tablespoons of the vegetable oil in a medium nonstick skillet over medium heat.

4. Working in batches and adding more oil as needed, pan-fry the pancakes, using 3 to 4 tablespoons batter per pancake. Flip each pancake once, and cook until golden, for a total 8 to 10 minutes each. Transfer to paper towels to drain.

5. Stir the soy sauce and vinegar together in a small bowl to make a dipping sauce.

6. To serve, you can cut the pancakes in half or in quarters if you wish. Serve with the soy sauce dip on the side.

SUBSTITUTION TIP: You can easily make a great vegetarian version of this recipe by removing the pork from the ingredient list.

COLORFUL COLD SOBA SALAD

쟁반국수 *jaengban guksu*

Jaengban guksu is good with a variety of different vegetables and meat. You can add chicken, beef, or pork for a hearty dish and seasonal vegetables for a fresh, light meal. Almost any fresh vegetables will work in this dish. *Serves 6 as a side dish*

PREP TIME: 20 MINUTES / COOK TIME: 10 MINUTES

Vegetarian-Friendly, Vegan-Friendly

6 ounces soba noodles

⅓ cup chicken broth

3 tablespoons soy sauce

2 tablespoons rice wine vinegar

2 tablespoons sugar

2 tablespoons toasted sesame oil

1 cup mesclun greens or thinly sliced red and green leaf lettuce

1 seeded English cucumber or 2 kirby cucumbers, thinly sliced

½ red bell pepper, thinly sliced

½ Asian pear, thinly sliced

¼ red onion, thinly sliced

1. Cook the soba noodles according to package directions.

2. While the noodles are cooking, in a small bowl, mix together the broth, soy sauce, vinegar, sugar, and sesame oil.

3. Drain the noodles and rinse in cold water. Drain very well, lining a colander with paper towels if needed. Let cool a bit.

4. In sections on a circular serving platter, arrange the greens, cucumber, bell pepper, Asian pear, and red onion. Place the soba noodles in a heap in the center of the platter.

5. Just before serving, pour the dressing over the salad.

SUBSTITUTION TIP: To make a vegan or vegetarian version, use vegetable broth in the dressing instead of chicken broth.

SEAWEED ROLLS

김밥 *kimbap*

Most people call these Korean rice rolls sushi, because at first glance, they do resemble the Japanese rolls that Westerners think of as sushi. But Korean rolls usually don't include raw fish. Traditional kimbap fillings include seasoned vegetables, egg, meat and/or imitation crabmeat, but these days, fillings range from cheesy to spicy to fresh. Kimbap is like the Korean version of a sandwich—you can change the filling to fit any diet, palate, or occasion. These are a popular snack, picnic, and lunchbox food in Korea. *Serves 4*

PREP TIME: 30 MINUTES / COOK TIME: 40 MINUTES

Vegetarian-Friendly

2 teaspoons toasted sesame oil

2 teaspoons salt

2 cups cooked rice, cooled

4 sheets nori (dried seaweed)

Traditional fillings (choose 1 or more)

1 carrot, julienned, quickly stir-fried with a pinch of salt

2 small cucumbers, seeded and cut into long strips, quickly stir-fried with a pinch of salt

2 eggs, whisked and cooked into a flat omelet and then cut into long strips

¾ cup cooked beef (*bulgogi*)

½ pound of spinach, blanched

½ cup yellow pickled radish (called danmuji or takuan), cut into strips

Imitation crab

Fish cake

VARIATION TIP: Other popular fillings include smoked salmon, kimchi, SPAM, tuna salad, and cheese.

1. Stir the sesame oil and salt into the cooled rice.

2. Lay the dried seaweed sheets shiny-side down on a bamboo sushi roller or a piece of aluminum foil. Spread about ½ cup rice over two-thirds of the seaweed, leaving the top one-third bare (moisten your fingers or a spoon to prevent the rice from sticking as you pat it down).

3. Lay your choice of fillings in a horizontal line about one-third of the way up from the bottom of the seaweed.

4. Roll the kimbap up from the bottom (like a jelly roll), pressing down to keep the roll tight and keep the fillings inside. As you roll, pull down toward the ends of the bamboo mat.

5. Spread a tiny dab of water along the top seam to seal the roll together. Set the roll aside and repeat to make the other rolls.

6. To serve, cut each roll into 7 or 8 rounds.

CANDIED SWEET POTATOES WITH WALNUTS

고구마맛탕 *goguma mattang*

A sweet treat and snack all kids (and adults) love, these candied sweet potatoes are easy to make. The traditional way to make this is to deep-fry the potatoes, but I like to steam and then pan-fry them for a healthier version. Korean sweet potatoes have white flesh and purple skin and are very sweet and nutty, but you can use orange sweet potatoes instead and the dish will still taste wonderful. *Serves 4 as a side dish*

PREP TIME: 5 MINUTES / COOK TIME: 10 MINUTES

Vegetarian-Friendly,
Vegan-Friendly, Gluten-Free

2 Korean sweet potatoes,
    peeled and cut into ¼-inch cubes

4 tablespoons sugar

4 tablespoons honey

1 tablespoon chopped walnuts (optional)

1 teaspoon black sesame seeds,
    for garnish (optional)

1. Steam the sweet potatoes in a covered metal steamer over boiling water for 8 minutes or until fork-tender.

2. While the potatoes are steaming, put the sugar in a small saucepan over medium-low heat and cook, stirring frequently, until it becomes liquid, 3 to 5 minutes. Add the honey, stir to combine, and then remove from the heat.

3. Fry the sweet potatoes for about 2 minutes over medium-high heat in a dry nonstick skillet that is large enough to fit them all. This will make them crispy.

4. In a medium bowl, toss together the fried potatoes, the sugar-honey syrup, and the nuts, if using.

5. Serve warm, garnished with the sesame seeds, if using.

SUBSTITUTION TIP: For a vegan version, omit the honey and add ½ tablespoon of agave syrup and an additional 2 tablespoons sugar.

RAMEN AND SPICY RICE CAKES

라볶이 *rabokki*

This dish combines two delicious, savory food items in one, ramen and spicy rice cakes (*tteokbokki*). It's surprisingly easy to make at home. I'll never forget the first time I tasted this dish. It was a chilly, rainy day, and my cousins had brought me to a tiny hole-in-the-wall restaurant in Seoul. The woman put this amazing street food combination in front of me, and it was an instant mood lifter! Korean rice cakes are made from a very sticky rice flour called *chapsal* that is steamed and then pounded into different shapes. These cylindrical rice cakes are available in Korean markets and online. *Serves 4*

PREP TIME: 10 MINUTES / COOK TIME: 40 MINUTES

♦♦♦

Vegetarian-Friendly

½ pound Korean cylindrical rice cakes (about one-fourth package)

1 large flat Korean fish cake sheet (*omuk*), cut into squares or rectangles

½ tablespoon vegetable oil

½ carrot, thinly sliced

½ sweet onion, thinly sliced

3 cups water

1 teaspoon soy sauce

¼ cup gochujang

1½ tablespoons sugar

1 package Korean instant ramen noodles (Shin Ramen brand), broken into pieces

2 scallions, sliced into 1-inch pieces

2 hard-boiled eggs, halved (optional)

SUBSTITUTION TIP: I love this dish super spicy, but you can reduce the amount of gochujang you use to make a less spicy dish.

1. If the rice cakes or fish cakes are frozen, thaw them in warm water and drain.

2. In a stockpot or large skillet over medium-high heat, heat the vegetable oil. Add carrot and onion and stir-fry them until slightly softened, 3 to 4 minutes.

3. Add the rice cakes, fish cakes, and water and raise the heat to high. When the water boils, reduce the heat to medium.

4. Stir in the soy sauce, gochujang, and sugar. When the sauce starts to thicken, add the noodles.

5. Cook the noodles until tender, according to the directions on the package, stirring occasionally and adding a little more water if necessary. When the noodles are tender, add the scallions and remove from the heat.

6. Before serving, add half an egg to each bowl (if using).

TOFU WITH SAUTÉED KIMCHI

두부김치 *dubu kimchi*

Dubu kimchi is both a popular Korean drinking snack (*anju*) and a delicious, easy way to use leftover kimchi. It's a perfectly balanced dish, because the flavorful sautéed kimchi is mellowed by the soft, delicate taste of the boiled or steamed tofu. *Serves 4*

PREP TIME: 5 MINUTES / COOK TIME: 15 MINUTES

Vegetarian-Friendly

2 teaspoons vegetable oil

½ cup thinly sliced pork (or bacon), cut into 1-inch pieces

3 garlic cloves, minced

1 cup Napa Cabbage Kimchi (page 54), roughly chopped into 1-inch pieces (older, aged kimchi is best)

2 teaspoons sugar

1 teaspoon soy sauce

1 teaspoon sesame seeds

1 teaspoon toasted sesame oil

1 block (12- to 14-ounce package) firm tofu

SUBSTITUTION TIP: For a vegetarian version, simply omit the pork.

1. Coat a large skillet or wok with the vegetable oil and heat over medium-high heat. Add the pork and sauté until almost cooked through, about 5 minutes. Drain off excess oil if necessary.

2. Add the garlic and sauté for about 2 minutes, stirring constantly. Add the kimchi and sauté for about 5 minutes, or until it becomes a darker reddish brown. Add the sugar, soy sauce, sesame seeds, and sesame oil to the pan and cook, stirring, for about 1 minute. Remove from heat.

3. Meanwhile, bring a pot of water to a gentle boil. Add the whole tofu block and boil for 3 minutes. Drain the tofu well and pat it dry with a paper towel.

4. Gently cut the tofu into rectangles or squares.

5. To serve, arrange the tofu on a serving platter and top with the sautéed kimchi. Alternatively, you can place the sautéed kimchi in the center of serving plate and arrange the tofu around it.

SPICY STIR-FRIED RICE CAKES

떡볶이 *tteokbokki*

This piping hot, super-spicy dish of cylindrical rice cakes (*duk*) is a popular street food in Korea. It is also eaten as a casual meal at home or as a snack with drinks. When I cook *tteokbokki* at home, I like to make it with fish cakes (*oden*, *omuk*), but you can also make it with beef or with no meat at all for a vegetarian version. I recommend napa cabbage as the main vegetable because it's widely available, but you can make it with bok choy or green cabbage, too. Feel free to experiment and change the vegetables to suit what you like or what you have at home. *Serves 4*

PREP TIME: 60 MINUTES / COOK TIME: 15 MINUTES

🌶🌶🌶

1 pound cylindrical rice cakes (*duk*), cut into 2-inch pieces

3 cups water, at room temperature

1 tablespoon gochujang

1 teaspoon gochugaru

1 tablespoon sugar

2 teaspoons minced garlic

1½ tablespoons soy sauce

1 cup rectangular fish cakes (*omuk*), cut into 1-inch pieces

3 shiitake mushrooms, soaked for 30 minutes, drained, and sliced into pieces

2 cups chopped napa cabbage

COOKING TIP: If you don't have time to soak the rice cakes in advance, you can add them into the pot at the very beginning when you are making the sauce and follow the rest of the recipe.

1. Soak the rice cakes in cold water for about an hour. Drain and set aside.

2. In a wide, shallow saucepan, mix 3 cups water with the gochujang, gochugaru, sugar, garlic, and soy sauce and bring to a boil over high heat. Add the fish cakes and stir to combine. Return to a boil and add the mushrooms, cabbage, and rice cakes. Bring up to a boil again and cook for about 3 minutes, and then turn off the heat. The sauce will thicken while it sits, but you can serve it immediately.

VARIATION TIP: A popular fusion dish in Korea is *tteokbokki carbonara*, or rice cakes in a creamy sauce that is like an Italian carbonara sauce. Add pancetta, 1 cup half-and-half, and ¼ cup grated Parmesan cheese to the sauce while cooking. For a less spicy version, omit the gochujang.

CHEESE CORN

Koreans love corn and they put it on pizzas, in pasta sauces, and in bread and cakes. This cheesy corn is a popular drinking snack (*anju*) and side dish at some Korean barbecue restaurants. Simple but satisfying, it is the Korean version of creamed corn. *Serves 4*

PREP TIME: 5 MINUTES / COOK TIME: 15 MINUTES

Vegetarian-Friendly, Gluten-Free

1 tablespoon butter, at room temperature, plus more for the baking dish

2 ears fresh sweet corn kernels or 2½ cups frozen sweet corn kernels, thawed and drained

⅓ cup mayonnaise

10 ounces mozzarella cheese, shredded

1 tablespoon sugar

Salt

Freshly ground black pepper

1 scallion, chopped, for garnish (optional)

1. Preheat the oven to 400°F.

2. Butter an 8-inch baking dish or loaf pan.

3. In a medium bowl, mix all the ingredients together well except the scallion, if using. Season with salt and pepper. Pour the mixture into the prepared baking dish.

4. Bake for 10 to 15 minutes, until the cheese is melted and the mixture is bubbling.

5. Serve immediately, garnished with chopped scallion (if using).

SERVING TIP: Although not traditional, this is a popular Korean side dish for grilled meats and casual meals. Try it at your next cookout and you won't have any leftovers.

CHEESE DONKATSU

치즈돈까스 *chijeu donkkaseu*

Donkatsu is a Japanese dish that is now popular in Korea. It was presumably introduced to the Korean peninsula in the early twentieth century during the Japanese occupation. When it originated in Japan, it was considered a fusion dish because it was the Japanese version of a European dish. Now it's part of the food culture in both Korea and Japan. This thin deep-fried cutlet is usually made with pork and served with shredded cabbage and a Japanese-style Worcestershire sauce (see Ingredient Tip following). You can also make it with beef or chicken and serve it with Western Worcestershire sauce. This recipe makes the dish the traditional way, with pork, but tops it with melted cheese. *Serves 2*

PREP TIME: 10 MINUTES / COOK TIME: 10 MINUTES

2 pork cutlets

1 egg, beaten

⅓ cup all-purpose flour

⅓ cup panko bread crumbs

Vegetable oil for deep-frying

⅓ cup grated mozzarella cheese

2 tablespoons donkatsu sauce, for drizzling

1. Pound the pork cutlets with a mallet or the back of a wooden spoon to make them as flat and thin as you can. It's easy to do this between two sheets of parchment paper, plastic wrap, or inside a zip-top plastic bag.

2. Put the egg and flour into two separate shallow bowls. Spread the panko bread crumbs on a clean cutting board or on a piece of parchment paper.

3. Dip the pork cutlets into the egg and then dredge them in the flour. Dip them into the egg again and then coat them thoroughly with the panko.

4. In a wok or heavy saucepan, heat 1 inch of vegetable oil over high heat. When the oil is very hot, add the cutlets and cook, turning once, until golden brown on both sides, about 3 minutes per side. Transfer the cutlets to a serving platter, and immediately sprinkle the mozzarella cheese over the top. Tent with foil or a pot lid to melt the cheese.

5. To serve, drizzle with donkatsu sauce.

VARIATION TIP: You can also make stuffed donkatsu, which is delicious. Get large spinach leaves and a slice of mozzarella cheese. Put the cheese on top of one side of the pork, cover with spinach leaves, and then coat with egg, flour, and panko before frying. Fry the side without cheese first, for 4 minutes. Then fry the cheesy side, for 2 minutes.

INGREDIENT TIP: Donkatsu sauce is Japanese-style Worcestershire sauce, and is made of unique blend of vegetables, Worcestershire sauce, and sugar. You can find this at Japanese and Korean markets and online. Mix equal parts ketchup and Worcestershire sauce at home if you don't have donkatsu sauce.

VARIATION TIP: For a change, serve this with Korean curry sauce instead of donkatsu sauce.

ROLLED OMELET

계란 말이 *gyeran mari*

Gyeran mari is as easy to make as an American omelet, but it looks gorgeous and is a hearty side dish for any meal. Healthy, delicious, and full of protein, this rolled omelet is good for picnics and lunchboxes because it is delicious at room temperature. Like most Korean dishes, this recipe has many variations. You can add different colorful vegetables, omit the seaweed if you don't have any, or Westernize it with the addition of some cheese. I usually cook this omelet in a very large skillet, but if you are using a standard-size skillet (10 to 12 inches), cook it in two batches. *Serves 3 as a side dish*

PREP TIME: 5 MINUTES / COOK TIME: 5 MINUTES

Vegetarian-Friendly, Gluten-Free

3 eggs

½ small onion, finely chopped

½ small carrot, finely chopped

1 teaspoon salt

1 sheet dried Korean roasted laver seaweed (*gim*)

1. In a medium bowl, whisk the eggs with the onion, carrot, and salt until well combined.

2. Heat a medium nonstick skillet over low heat. Add the egg mixture and heat slowly for 2 to 3 minutes, until almost cooked through, then place the seaweed sheet on top of the omelet. Roll the omelet into a tight roll by lifting one side with a flat wooden spatula. Turn the rolled omelet over and cook for an additional 1 to 2 minutes to make sure it is cooked through. Transfer to serving plate and let cool for a few minutes.

3. To serve, cut crosswise into 1-inch pieces and lay in cross-sections, like sushi rolls.

COOKING TIP: You can use a small amount of butter or oil, if desired, if you don't have a nonstick skillet.

BRAISED EGGS

계란장조림 *gyeran jangjorim*

These salty and sweet eggs are perfect for lunchboxes, snacks, and picnics. Although they are traditionally eaten as a side dish, you can make them the star of your lunch or dinner with the addition of just a bowl of rice and some soup. *Serves 3 as a side dish*

PREP TIME: 15 MINUTES / COOK TIME: 15 MINUTES

Vegetarian-Friendly

¼ cup soy sauce

2 tablespoons light brown sugar

1 cup water

2½ tablespoons mirin

1 scallion

6 hard-boiled eggs, peeled

1. In a small saucepan, mix together the soy sauce, brown sugar, water, mirin, and scallion and heat up over high heat, stirring occasionally. When the mixture comes to a rolling boil, remove the scallion (save for another use) and reduce the heat to medium.

2. Add the eggs to the soy sauce mixture and simmer gently for about 10 minutes. The sauce will reduce somewhat. Roll them around in the sauce with a wooden spoon while they simmer.

3. Transfer the eggs from the pan with slotted spoon to a shallow bowl, and let cool until cool enough to handle.

4. Carefully slice the eggs in half.

5. Store covered in the refrigerator for up to 3 days, before packing in lunch boxes.

SERVING TIP: Because you can eat these at room temperature, these tasty eggs are perfect for lunchboxes and picnic meals.

SPICY OCTOPUS

낙지볶음 *nakji bokkeum*

Octopus is everywhere in Korea, and since Koreans love the freshest seafood, you'll see tanks of live octopus in markets and restaurants everywhere. This spicy stir-fried octopus is a popular main dish, street food, and drinking snack enjoyed by Koreans of all ages. *Serves 4*

PREP TIME: 15 MINUTES, PLUS 15 MINUTES TO MARINATE / COOK TIME: 10 MINUTES

1 pound octopus, cleaned

2½ tablespoons gochujang

1½ tablespoons gochugaru

1 tablespoon low-sodium soy sauce

1½ tablespoons toasted sesame oil

1 tablespoon sesame seeds

2 tablespoons minced garlic

½ sweet onion, sliced

2 scallions, cut into 1-inch pieces

½ medium carrot, thinly sliced

2 green chiles, like jalapeño, seeded and thinly sliced

1. Cut the octopus legs into 2-inch pieces and quarter the head. Rinse and dry.

2. In a large bowl, mix together the gochujang, gochugaru, soy sauce, sesame oil, sesame seeds, and garlic to make the sauce.

3. Add the octopus to the sauce and mix to combine. Let marinate for 10 to 15 minutes.

4. In a large skillet or stir-fry pan over medium-high heat, cook the octopus, onion, scallions, carrot, and chiles until the octopus changes color and is cooked through, 7 to 10 minutes. Make sure not to overcook it.

VARIATION TIP: To make this a one-dish dinner, serve it on top of a bed of white rice.

PORK BONE SOUP

감자탕 *gamjatang*

Super-hearty, rich, and delicious, long-simmered pork bone soup is the supreme comfort food for winter evenings or late-night drinking. Like Italian osso bucco, this soup gets its richness from bone marrow, so you really need to use pork bones to make this dish successful. *Serves 6*

PREP TIME: 90 MINUTES / COOK TIME: 2 HOURS

Gluten-Free

6 to 8 sliced pork neck bones

¼ cup peeled sliced fresh ginger, plus 1 tablespoon minced

10 cups water

1 large sweet onion, sliced

2 dried shiitake mushrooms, thinly sliced

2 tablespoons doenjang

2 small Korean green chiles, seeded and sliced

6 to 8 garlic cloves, minced

2 tablespoons fish sauce

3 tablespoons mirin

1 tablespoon gochujang

2 tablespoons gochugaru

4 large potatoes, peeled and quartered

¼ small napa cabbage, sliced into large chunks

2 scallions, cut into 1-inch pieces

Freshly ground black pepper

INGREDIENT TIP: For extra flavor, add some perilla leaves (*kkaennip*) and chrysanthemum leaves (*sukgat*), which are widely used in Korean, Japanese, and Chinese cooking.

1. In a large bowl, soak the pork bones in cold water for 1 to 2 hours to draw out some of the blood. Drain and rinse the bones.

2. Put the bones and ginger slices in a large stockpot and cover with water. Bring to a boil over high heat. As soon as the water boils, remove the pot from the heat, drain, and discard the ginger slices.

3. Rinse the pot, return the bones to the pot, and add the 10 cups water. Bring to a boil over high heat. Add the onion, mushrooms, minced ginger, and doenjang. Reduce the heat to medium-low, and simmer for 1½ hours.

4. While the bones are simmering, in a small bowl, mix together the chiles, garlic, fish sauce, mirin, gochujang, and gochugaru.

5. Remove the mushrooms from the stockpot, which have now been reconstituted, and slice them, and return to the pot. Add the sauce mixture, potatoes, cabbage, and scallions. Simmer for 30 more minutes.

6. Season with pepper just before serving hot.

KOREAN-STYLE SWEET AND SOUR PORK

탕수육 *tangsuyuk*

This pork dish is a Koreanized Chinese recipe, and it's similar to Americanized Chinese sweet and sour dishes. It is a popular snack, kids' food, special occasion dish, and drinking snack in Korea. *Serves 4*

PREP TIME: 15 MINUTES, PLUS 1 HOUR FOR SOAKING / COOK TIME: 15 MINUTES

1 cup cornstarch, plus 2 tablespoons

2 cups water, divided

1 egg, lightly beaten

1 tablespoon lower-sodium soy sauce

2 tablespoons rice vinegar

5 tablespoons sugar

1 tablespoon mirin

Peanut oil for deep-frying

12 ounces pork, fat trimmed, cut into thin strips

½ onion, sliced

¼ carrot, sliced

½ small cucumber, sliced

1 teaspoon toasted sesame oil

Salt

Freshly ground black pepper

1. In a small bowl, stir together 1 cup cornstarch and 1 cup water. Let sit for 1 hour. The cornstarch will have settled and separated from the water. Pour off the water from the top.

2. Add the egg to the cornstarch mixture and whisk to combine. Set aside.

3. In a small bowl, mix together the remaining 1 cup water, soy sauce, vinegar, sugar, and mirin and stir to combine. Set the sauce aside.

4. Heat about 2 inches of the peanut oil in a large saucepan or wok over high heat.

5. Dip the pork strips in the cornstarch-egg mixture and use your hands to coat the meat. Drop the battered pork in batches into the hot oil and deep-fry until it is golden. Drain on paper towels.

6. Once all of the pork strips have been fried, deep-fry them again to make them extra crispy. Drain on paper towels.

7. In a dry medium sauté pan over medium-high heat, sauté the onion, carrot, cucumber, sesame oil, seasoned with salt and pepper, for 2 minutes. Add the sauce mixture, stir to combine, and bring to a boil.

8. Meanwhile, in a small bowl, mix 2 tablespoons water with the remaining 2 tablespoons cornstarch to make a slurry. Just when sauce starts to boil, add the cornstarch slurry to the sauce and cook, stirring, until it starts to thicken. Reduce the heat to low and simmer for about 5 minutes.

9. To serve, arrange the pork pieces on a serving platter and pour the sauce over the top of the pork.

VARIATION TIP: You can sweeten this dish more by adding some pineapple or apple chunks to the sauce in the last couple minutes of cooking.

Chapter Six

SIDE DISHES

Korean meals usually include rice, a hot soup or stew, kimchi, and a number of vegetable, seafood, or meat side dishes. The more celebratory or formal the meal, the more side dishes are served, and meals for special occasions will have a dozen or more dishes on the table. Everyday family meals usually include about three side dishes, along with rice, kimchi, and soup or stew.

Most of the side dishes in this chapter are traditionally part of a larger Korean meal, but you can make some of the heartier salads for a light lunch or meal. Some of these recipes make four servings, so you might want to double those if you are using them as part of a Western-style meal of one main dish, one side dish, and a salad.

SEASONED BABY BOK CHOY

겉절이 *geotjeori*

When I can find nice baby bok choy, this dish is one of my favorite things to make. It's a delicious kimchi that is ready immediately—you don't have to wait for it to pickle or ferment! I love when baby bok choy is in season, because it has all the great Korean flavors but tastes and feels very fresh. A lot of the bok choy in non-Asian groceries is large, and even the "baby" bok choy is not small. Since the large bok choy is more fibrous, I tend to use it in stir-fries, not in this kimchi dish. *Serves 6 as a side dish*

PREP TIME: 15 MINUTES, PLUS 1 HOUR 20 MINUTES FOR SALTING / COOK TIME: 0

Vegetarian-Friendly, Vegan-Friendly

½ pound baby bok choy

½ cup sea salt

1 tablespoon gochugaru

1 teaspoon toasted sesame oil

2 teaspoons fish sauce

1 teaspoon sugar

1 teaspoon minced garlic

1 sweet onion, sliced into strips

1 green chile, like jalapeño, seeded and sliced into strips

½ red bell pepper, seeded and sliced into strips

2 scallions, cut into slivers

1 tablespoon toasted sesame seeds

1. Make sure the bok choy is dry. Put it in a large bowl, and sprinkle it with the salt. Add room-temperature water to cover the bok choy. Soak for about 1 hour. Transfer to a colander in the sink and let drain for 15 to 20 minutes.

2. Meanwhile, in a large mixing bowl, stir together the gochugaru, sesame oil, fish sauce, sugar, and garlic.

3. Add the bok choy to the sauce mixture and toss to coat thoroughly.

4. Add the onion, jalapeño, bell pepper, scallions, and sesame seeds and mix everything together well.

5. Serve immediately.

SEASONED RADISH STRIPS

무생채 *musaengchae*

Musaengchae is a fresh Korean radish salad that goes well with savory stews and well-seasoned sautéed dishes. *Saengchae* is a general term for side dishes made with uncooked vegetables. This dish goes perfectly with mixed rice dishes and as a topping for cold noodles. *Serves 6 as a side dish*

PREP TIME: 45 MINUTES / COOK TIME: 0

Vegetarian-Friendly, Vegan-Friendly

1 small Korean radish or
    2 daikon radishes,
    cut into matchsticks

2 teaspoons salt

2 teaspoons gochugaru

1 tablespoon rice wine vinegar

2 tablespoons sugar

¼ teaspoon minced peeled fresh ginger

1 tablespoon sesame seeds

1 tablespoon chopped scallion

1. Put the radish in a medium bowl and mix with the salt. Let stand for 15 minutes. Drain and squeeze tightly in your hands to drain out any liquid.

2. In a large bowl, mix together the radish and gochugaru. Add the vinegar, sugar, ginger, sesame seeds, and scallion, and mix together gently to combine.

3. Serve immediately.

INGREDIENT TIP: You can also add carrot strips and/or red pepper strips to the finished dish for added texture and color.

COOKING TIP: If you don't have time to salt the radish first, then you can skip this step, but the end result won't be as crunchy.

SEASONED BLACK SOYBEANS

콩자반 *kongjaban*

A sweet and nutty side dish, these seasoned black soy beans are delicious
and easy to make. You can also use this recipe to make other kinds of
seasoned beans. This is an essential side dish (*mit banchan*), and is popular
in everyday meals and lunchboxes (dosirak). *Serves 8 as a side dish*

PREP TIME: 4 HOURS FOR SOAKING / COOK TIME: 30 MINUTES

Vegetarian-Friendly, Vegan-Friendly

1 cup black soybeans, soaked
    for at least 4 hours

1 cup water

½ cup soy sauce

½ cup sugar

1 tablespoon toasted sesame oil

1 teaspoon sesame seeds (optional)

1. In a small saucepan over medium-high
heat, combine the soybeans and water
and bring to a boil. Cook for 15 minutes.

2. Reduce the heat to medium-low, and
stir in the soy sauce, sugar, and sesame
oil. Cook for 10 to 15 minutes. Remove
from the heat and stir in the sesame seeds
(if using).

3. Serve warm, cold, or at room
temperature.

SUBSTITUTION TIP: You can use canned
black soy beans if you don't have time to
soak dry beans.

SEASONED SPINACH

시금치나물 *sigeumchi namul*

This seasoned spinach is a light Korean side dish that can also be used in other Korean main dishes like stir-fried noodles, rice and seaweed rolls (kimbap), and rice mixed with vegetables (bibimbap). It's a basic and essential Korean side dish (*mit banchan*), and one of the most common *namul* dishes, which are cooked and lightly seasoned vegetable side dishes that can be made from greens, roots, or herbs. *Serves 5 as a side dish*

PREP TIME: 5 MINUTES / COOK TIME: 10 MINUTES

Vegetarian-Friendly, Vegan-Friendly

1 pound fresh spinach

2 tablespoons soy sauce

1 tablespoon toasted sesame oil

1 tablespoon sesame seeds

2 teaspoons sesame salt (see Ingredient Tip)

2 garlic cloves, finely chopped

2 teaspoons sugar

1. Bring a medium saucepan of water to a boil over high heat. Drop in the spinach and blanch for 30 seconds until wilted. Drain in a colander and rinse with cold water to stop the cooking. Gently squeeze to remove excess water.

2. In a medium bowl, mix the spinach with the soy sauce, sesame oil, sesame seeds, sesame salt, garlic, and sugar and toss to combine.

3. Serve warm or at room temperature.

INGREDIENT TIP: Sesame salt is popular condiment in Korean and Japanese cooking and is used in marinades, seasonings, and as a topping for stews and vegetable dishes. You can find it in Korean grocery stores and online. If you don't have sesame salt, you can add 1 teaspoon of salt and an additional 1 teaspoon soy sauce.

SEASONED EGGPLANT

Gaji namul is a simple, tasty Korean side dish made of steamed eggplant strips and seasonings. This recipe is best when you use fresh summer eggplant, but you can also make it at any time of year when you find good eggplant. Just like with other seasoned vegetables (namul), you can use this as a component of mixed rice dishes (bibimbap) and mixed noodle dishes. *Serves 4 as a side dish*

PREP TIME: 5 MINUTES / COOK TIME: 10 MINUTES

Vegetarian-Friendly, Vegan-Friendly

2 medium Asian eggplant

2 scallions, finely chopped

2 garlic cloves, minced

2 tablespoons soy sauce

1 teaspoon toasted sesame oil

¼ teaspoon sugar

1 teaspoon gochugaru

1 teaspoon toasted sesame seeds

Pinch of salt

Freshly ground black pepper

1. Wash and cut the eggplant in half and then crosswise into quarters. You might have to cut it again if you have long eggplant. Then cut into 2-inch strips.

2. Put the eggplant in a steamer basket set over boiling water and steam until fork-tender, 5 to 10 minutes. Transfer to a large bowl.

3. Add the scallions, garlic, soy sauce, sesame oil, sugar, gochugaru, sesame seeds, and salt, and season with pepper.

4. Cool to room temperature before serving.

SUBSTITUTION TIP: You can use other types of eggplant to make this dish, but the best option if you can't find Asian varieties is Italian eggplant because they have thin skins. If you are going to use the big globe eggplants that are more common in America, peel them first.

EGG-BATTERED ZUCCHINI

호박전 *hobakjeon*

A delicious and healthy Korean side dish, these pan-fried zucchini medallions are easy to prepare and go well with almost every Korean meal. To make these, zucchini slices are coated in a thin batter of flour and egg, sautéed on both sides, and served with a seasoned soy sauce for dipping. *Jun* (also *jeon* or *chon*) are a pancakelike pan-fried Korean dish. They can be made from almost any ingredients, including meat, seafood, vegetables, and kimchi. *Serves 4 as a side dish*

PREP TIME: 5 MINUTES / COOK TIME: 15 MINUTES

Vegetarian-Friendly

2 teaspoons salt, divided

2 medium zucchini, sliced into ¼-inch coins

2 eggs, beaten

½ cup all-purpose flour

1 tablespoon vegetable oil

Seasoned Soy Sauce (page 49), for dipping

VARIATION TIP: You can use this egg-battered technique with many different vegetables, including bell peppers, potatoes, sweet potatoes, and onions.

1. In a medium bowl, sprinkle 1 teaspoon salt over the zucchini slices.

2. Add the remaining teaspoon of salt to the beaten eggs in a small bowl and stir with a fork to combine.

3. Put the flour and the egg mixture in separate shallow bowls next to the stove.

4. Heat the vegetable oil in a sauté pan over medium heat.

5. Dredge the zucchini coins in the flour, and then dip them in the beaten egg to coat. Put the coated zucchini slices into the hot pan. Cook, turning once, until they are a light golden brown, for 3 to 4 minutes per side.

6. Serve with seasoned soy sauce alongside for dipping.

GARLIC CHIVE SALAD

부추오이무침 *buchuoi muchim*

This Garlic Chive Salad is snappy, spicy, and fresh. It adds zest to any meal, and is an excellent side dish with grilled beef, steamed tofu, and dumpling soup. It is one of my favorite additions to mixed rice (bibimbap) during the summer months. Garlic chives are flatter than Western chives and taste like a combination of garlic and chives. If you cannot find garlic chives (*buchu*) but you still want to make an oniony salad, you can use a combination of finely sliced scallions, onions, and chives. *Serves 4 as a side dish*

PREP TIME: 5 MINUTES / COOK TIME: 0

Vegetarian-Friendly, Vegan-Friendly

2 cups 2-inch pieces garlic chives

1 tablespoon soy sauce

1 tablespoon white vinegar

2 teaspoons gochugaru

1 tablespoons sugar

1 tablespoon toasted sesame oil

1 teaspoon toasted sesame seeds (optional)

1. In a medium bowl, mix all of the ingredients together with the sesame seeds (if using), tossing well to combine.

2. Serve at room temperature.

TIP: You can easily grow garlic chives in your garden, as they are hardy and grow well. Their aroma also helps keeps the bugs at bay.

SERVING TIP: This is not date food! Your breath will be strong after eating it.

COLD CUCUMBER SOUP

오이냉국 *oi naengguk*

Crisp, refreshing, and icy cold, this cucumber soup is the perfect side dish in a meal for a hot summer day. Sometimes called *oi naengchae*, this iced cucumber soup is best when made with crisp, fresh cucumbers. *Serves 6 as a side dish*

PREP TIME: 15 MINUTES, PLUS 10 MINUTES FOR SOAKING AND 30 MINUTES FOR CHILLING / COOK TIME: 0

Vegetarian-Friendly,
Vegan-Friendly, Gluten-Free

3 small kirby cucumbers or pickling cucumbers, cut into matchsticks

1 teaspoon gochugaru

¼ cup apple cider vinegar

1 tablespoon sugar

2 tablespoons soy sauce

1 tablespoon toasted sesame oil

4 cups water

Ice cubes, for serving

2 teaspoons toasted sesame seeds (optional)

1. In a large bowl, mix the cucumbers with the gochugaru, vinegar, sugar, soy sauce, and sesame oil. Let sit in the seasoning mixture for 10 minutes.

2. Add the water to the bowl and stir to combine.

3. Chill in the refrigerator for at least 30 minutes.

4. To serve, ladle the soup into small bowls, add a few ice cubes to each, and sprinkle with sesame seeds (if using).

INGREDIENT TIP: If you have thin-skinned cucumbers, you don't have to peel them. If your cucumbers have waxy, thick skins, then it's best to peel them. Kirby cucumbers are best, Persian cucumbers work really well, and English cukes are a good third choice.

COLD TOFU SALAD

This is an easy, delicious salad that you can make in less than 10 minutes. It uses a whole package of tofu, so it's a good lunch or quick meal for two. I like to keep this salad simple, with greens, red bell peppers, and slivered scallions, but you can enhance it with other vegetables. *Serves 3*

PREP TIME: 15 MINUTES / COOK TIME: 5 MINUTES

Vegetarian-Friendly, Vegan-Friendly

1 (12- to 14-ounce) package firm tofu

2 tablespoons lower-sodium soy sauce

1 tablespoon rice wine vinegar

1 teaspoon light brown sugar

2 teaspoons toasted sesame oil

1 teaspoon gochugaru

4 ounces mesclun or spring salad mix

3 scallions, sliced into thin strips

½ red bell pepper, cut into thin strips

1 teaspoon black sesame seeds, for garnish

SUBSTITUTION TIP: If you don't have time or the ingredients to make your own dressing, any soy-based store-bought dressing will work on this salad.

1. Steam the tofu in the microwave by placing the whole block on a microwave-safe plate and covering it loosely with a damp paper towel. Cook for 4 minutes on 80 percent power.

2. Remove from the microwave and let sit for 2 to 3 minutes under the paper towel. Drain and rinse under cold water to cool. (Alternatively, you can steam the tofu in a steamer basket over boiling water on the stovetop for 5 minutes, and then rinse with cold water to cool.)

3. Slice the steamed tofu into rectangles and squares.

4. In a small bowl, whisk together the soy sauce, vinegar, brown sugar, sesame oil, and gochugaru.

5. In a large bowl, add the mesclun, scallions, and bell pepper and toss with half of the dressing.

6. Place the dressed vegetables on a large serving platter and arrange the steamed tofu on top.

7. To serve, drizzle the remaining half of the dressing over the tofu, and garnish with the sesame seeds.

SEAWEED AND CUCUMBER SALAD

Crisp cucumbers and flavorful seaweed make for a healthy, refreshing side salad. This is called *sunomono* in Japanese and *miyuk muchim* in Korean. I sometimes garnish it with gochugaru for a bit of spice. *Serves 4 as a side dish*

PREP TIME: 15 MINUTES, PLUS 15 MINUTES FOR SOAKING / COOK TIME: 0

Vegetarian-Friendly,
Vegan-Friendly, Gluten-Free

1 cup dried wakame seaweed (*miyuk*)

3 cups water

1 kirby cucumber or pickling
     cucumber, cut into thin slices

¼ small red onion, very finely sliced

2 tablespoons apple cider vinegar

1 tablespoon sugar

1 tablespoon salt

1. Put the seaweed in a small bowl and cover it with the water. Soak for 15 minutes.

2. Drain the seaweed, and if it's not already in small pieces, then cut into 1-inch pieces.

3. In a large bowl, combine the seaweed, cucumber, and onion.

4. For the dressing, in a small bowl, whisk together the vinegar, sugar, and salt.

5. Pour the dressing over the vegetables and toss to combine.

6. Serve at room temperature or chilled.

INGREDIENT TIP: If you can't find kirby cucumbers, use pickling or Persian cucumbers. If you can't find those, then use one-fourth of an English cucumber, seeded.

SPICY GREEN BEANS

These slightly spicy green beans may be influenced by Chinese cooking, but Korean home cooks stir-fry all types of vegetables in different sauces. Korean cuisine is vegetable-heavy, and there are countless ways to prepare different types of vegetables. *Serves 8 as a side dish*

PREP TIME: 15 MINUTES / COOK TIME: 10 MINUTES

Vegetarian-Friendly, Vegan-Friendly

2 tablespoons vegetable oil

2 pounds whole green beans, trimmed

1 tablespoon minced garlic

2 teaspoons minced peeled fresh ginger

1 teaspoon salt

3 tablespoons soy sauce

1 tablespoon sugar

1 teaspoon gochugaru

1. In a large skillet, stir-fry pan, or wok, heat the vegetable oil over medium heat.

2. Stir-fry the green beans, garlic, and ginger until the beans are crisp-tender, 5 to 6 minutes.

3. Reduce the heat to medium-low and stir in the salt, soy sauce, sugar, and gochugaru. Stir-fry for another 2 minutes.

4. Serve hot.

SUBSTITUTION TIP: Since this is so quick and easy, you can use this recipe as a base for different types of vegetables, from cabbage to kale to zucchini.

STEAMED EGG

계란찜 *gyeran jjim*

You can make this quick and easy steamed egg dish (*gyeran jjim*) in the micro-wave or on top of the stove. Koreans enjoy eggs at any meal of the day, so this steamed egg is a side dish for morning, noon, or night. *Serves 4 as a side dish*

PREP TIME: 2 MINUTES / COOK TIME: 10 MINUTES

Vegetarian-Friendly

4 eggs

¾ cup water

2 teaspoons salt

1 scallion, chopped

1. In a small heat-safe bowl (porcelain or glass), whisk together the eggs, water, salt, and scallion until fully combined. If using the microwave, cover the bowl with a microwave-safe plate and cook on high heat for 4 minutes. If steaming on the stove, place the bowl in a steamer over medium-low heat and steam for 10 minutes over simmering water.

2. Serve warm in the center of the table as a shared side dish.

COOKING TIP: If you don't have a big enough steamer to hold the bowl, you can put the bowl in a large lidded saucepan with a few inches of water at the bottom. Steam fort 15 minutes over medium-low heat.

SOY SAUCED POTATOES

감자조림 *gamja jorim*

This quick and easy recipe for stir-fried potatoes in a delicious sauce is called *gamja jorim* in Korean. It can be spicy if you use Korean chiles or jalapeños with a lot of heat, or you can also use red or green bell peppers if you don't want any spice. If you use red potatoes, you can keep the peel on and just scrub them well before cutting them up. *Serves 6*

PREP TIME: 10 MINUTES / COOK TIME: 10 MINUTES

Vegetarian-Friendly, Vegan-Friendly

2 tablespoons vegetable oil

1¼ pounds potatoes, peeled and cut into thin slices or small cubes

1 tablespoon toasted sesame oil

2 tablespoons sugar

¼ cup soy sauce

1 tablespoon minced garlic

5 tablespoons water

½ teaspoon freshly ground black pepper

5 small green Korean chiles, seeded and cut into 1-inch pieces

Pinch of toasted sesame seeds, for garnish (optional)

1. Heat the vegetable oil in a large skillet over medium heat.

2. Add the potatoes and stir-fry for 2 to 3 minutes.

3. Add the sesame oil, sugar, soy sauce, garlic, water, and pepper and reduce the heat to low. Cover and simmer for 3 to 4 minutes.

4. Add the chiles and cook for 2 to 3 more minutes, until the potatoes are cooked through.

5. To serve, add the sesame seeds and toss to mix (if using).

INGREDIENT TIP: You can also make this with unpeeled, scrubbed baby potatoes.

ROASTED KABOCHA SQUASH

All different types of sweet potato and squash are beloved in Korean cuisine, and they are used in everything from porridges to stews and desserts. This simple roasted squash dish can be a snack or part of a meal. Kabocha squash is soft and naturally sweet. It is seasonal, so grab them when you see them in the fall. *Serves 4 as a side dish*

PREP TIME: 10 MINUTES / COOK TIME: 30 MINUTES

Vegetarian-Friendly, Gluten-Free

1 small kabocha squash, halved and seeded

2 tablespoons butter, at room temperature

1 tablespoon honey, plus more if desired

Salt

1. Preheat the oven to 400°F.

2. Line a baking sheet with aluminum foil or parchment paper.

3. Cut the squash into wedges or chunks and put on the baking sheet, cut-side up. Dot the squash with the butter and drizzle the honey over the top.

4. Bake for about 30 minutes, turning once, or until the squash is soft.

5. Before serving hot, season with salt and more honey, if you like it sweeter.

INGREDIENT TIP: Although butter is not a traditional part of Korean cuisine, today Koreans do use it in dishes like this one to add flavor. This is a delicious, simple way to prepare a traditional Korean vegetable.

SWEET POTATO TEMPURA

Koreans enjoy all different kinds of tempura. A good tempura dish
is neither oily nor heavy. It doesn't seem anything like fast food,
even though it is deep fried. Sweet potato tempura is delicious, but
you can also make this recipe with regular potatoes. *Serves 2*

PREP TIME: 15 MINUTES / COOK TIME: 10 MINUTES

Vegetarian-Friendly, Vegan-Friendly

2 medium sweet potatoes, scrubbed
Vegetable or peanut oil for cooking
½ cup tempura flour
¼ cup very cold water

INGREDIENT TIP: Tempura flour is a packaged mix used to make tempura. It's
usually a mixture of wheat flour, starch
(potato or corn), baking powder, and
salt. You can find this in Asian markets
and online.

1. Cut the sweet potato into thin slices and
soak in a large bowl of water for 5 minutes. Drain and pat dry with paper towels
to make sure they are very dry.

2. Put about 2 inches of peanut oil (use
an oil that has a high smoke point) into
a deep, heavy-bottomed skillet or wok
and heat it to 375°F (use a thermometer
to check).

3. Make the tempura batter in a small
bowl by combining the tempura flour
with the cold water and mixing gently.

4. Dip the sweet potato slices with batter,
coating them, and slide gently into the hot
oil. Don't overcrowd the oil while cooking.
When the sweet potato pieces begin to
float up to the surface, gently turn each
piece over and cook the other side. When
they're done (about 1 minute per side),
drain them on paper towels.

5. Serve hot.

SCALLION SALAD

파무침 *pa muchim*

If you've ever been to a Korean barbecue restaurant, then you'll recognize this scallion side salad that is often served alongside grilled meat and seafood dishes. You can add it to your lettuce wraps or just treat it as another side dish or salad. *Serves 4 as a side dish*

PREP TIME: 20 MINUTES / COOK TIME: 0

Vegetarian-Friendly, Vegan-Friendly

4 scallions, sliced lengthwise
    into super-fine strips

2 teaspoons toasted sesame oil

2 tablespoons extra-fine sugar

2 tablespoons rice vinegar

2 teaspoons gochugaru

Pinch of salt

1. Soak the scallions in very cold water for 10 minutes so they have a good crunch. Drain well, patting them dry with paper towels if needed.

2. In a large bowl, combine the scallions with the sesame oil, sugar, vinegar, gochugaru, and salt.

3. Serve at room temperature or chilled.

VARIATION TIP: This is wonderful side dish, and you can also save some to use in sandwiches.

BRAISED TOFU

두부조림 *dubu jorim*

This saucy, savory braised tofu is a hearty main dish or side dish and is
easy to make for weeknight dinners. It's one of the few Korean dishes
where tofu is the star of the show, and it's my go-to side dish if I'm hosting
a lot of vegetarians. This is also great for lunchboxes and picnics, since
it can be served cold or at room temperature. *Serves 3 as a side dish*

PREP TIME: 10 MINUTES / COOK TIME: 15 MINUTES

Vegetarian-Friendly, Vegan-Friendly

1 (12- to 14-ounce) block medium-firm tofu,
   cubed or cut into rectangular pieces

1 cup water

1 cup Anchovy Stock (page 46)

2 tablespoons soy sauce

1 tablespoon honey

1 garlic clove, minced

½ sweet onion, chopped

1 green chile, like jalapeño, seeded and sliced

1 red chile, like Korean or Spanish,
   seeded and sliced

1 tablespoon gochugaru

1 teaspoon toasted sesame seeds, for garnish

1. Put the tofu in a deep skillet over
medium-high heat. Add the water,
anchovy stock, and soy sauce. Stir in the
honey and garlic and bring to a simmer.
Reduce the heat to low, cover the pan, and
simmer gently for 5 minutes.

2. Add the onion, green chile, red chile,
and gochugaru, and stir to combine.
Simmer, uncovered, until the vegetables
are tender, 6 to 8 minutes.

3. Garnish with sesame seeds, and serve
hot or at room temperature.

SUBSTITUTION TIP: To make a vegan
version, omit the honey and substitute
½ tablespoon light brown sugar.

STIR-FRIED ANCHOVIES WITH PEPPERS

멸치볶음 *myeolchi bokkeum*

This Korean anchovy dish is easy, satisfying, and nutritious. It is full of crunch, calcium, and terrific flavor. *Serves 8 as a side dish*

PREP TIME: 3 MINUTES / COOK TIME: 10 MINUTES

1 tablespoon vegetable oil

2 cups dried small anchovies

1 green chile, like jalapeño, seeded and sliced into strips

2 tablespoons soy sauce

1 tablespoon honey

1 teaspoon toasted sesame seeds

2 teaspoons mirin

1 teaspoon toasted sesame oil

1. Heat the oil in a medium skillet over medium-high heat. Add the anchovies and chile and sauté for 3 minutes and then remove from the heat.

2. In a small saucepan over medium-high heat, stir together the soy sauce, honey, sesame seeds, mirin, and sesame oil and bring to a boil.

3. Add the sauce to the anchovy-chile mixture and stir-fry for 2 minutes, or until the sauce is well distributed.

4. Serve hot.

INGREDIENT TIP: You will find these small dried anchovies in Korean and Asian grocery stores.

TOSSED SALAD WITH SHRIMP, NOODLES, AND SPICY KOREAN DRESSING

Bright and fresh, this tossed salad is packed with vegetables, shrimp, and noodles and topped with a spicy-sweet dressing. You can increase the amount of pasta and shrimp if you want to serve this as a full meal. This Korean-style dressing is so good you can customize this salad in a hundred ways; feel free to change up the vegetables, protein, noodles, and nuts as you wish. *Serves 4*

PREP TIME: 20 MINUTES / COOK TIME: 10 MINUTES

4 to 6 ounces linguine

12 ounces medium shrimp, peeled and deveined

1 tablespoon light brown sugar

3 tablespoons lemon juice

2 tablespoons gochujang

2 tablespoons mayonnaise

1 teaspoon lower-sodium soy sauce

4 cups sliced red leaf lettuce, mesclun, or spring mix

1 cup thinly sliced red onion

⅓ cup matchstick-cut carrots

⅓ cup broken candied walnuts

1. Cook the noodles according to the directions on the package. Add the shrimp to the pot 3 minutes before the end of the cooking time. Drain the noodles and shrimp, rinse with cold water, and drain again. Line a colander with paper towels and let the noodles and shrimp drain in it for a few minutes to get rid of any excess water.

2. To make the dressing, in a large bowl, combine the brown sugar, lemon juice, gochujang, mayonnaise, and soy sauce and stir until the sugar dissolves.

3. Add the noodles, shrimp, lettuce, onion, and carrot to the dressing and toss to combine well.

4. To serve, plate the salad onto four plates and top each with some of the candied walnuts.

SUBSTITUTION TIP: You can also use soba, egg, or rice noodles instead of linguine.

SOY-BRAISED BEEF AND CHILES

장조림 *jangjorim*

This sensational Korean side dish is richly flavored from long simmering. The meat becomes tender and the chiles give the dish a spicy kick. For less heat, remove the seeds from the chiles before cooking them, or cut down the number of peppers you are using. I like my *jangjorim* to be on the salty and spicy side, but I have had sweeter versions that were delicious as well. If you prefer the sweet version, add more sugar and only a couple of peppers to the pot. *Serves 8 as a side dish*

PREP TIME: 35 MINUTES / COOK TIME: 2 HOURS

1 pound beef brisket, beef shank, or lean stew meat, cut into large chunks

4 cups water

1 cup soy sauce

¼ cup sugar

8 garlic cloves, peeled

8 green chiles, like Korean or jalapeño, sliced or left whole

3 or 4 medium hard-boiled eggs, shelled (optional)

1. In a large stockpot, stir together the meat, water, soy sauce, sugar, garlic, and chiles and mix well. Bring to a boil over high heat. Reduce the heat to low, cover the pot, and simmer gently for 1 to 2 hours, until the meat is tender.

2. Add the eggs to the pot (if using) 15 minutes before the end of cooking time. Remove the pot from the heat.

3. Transfer the meat to a cutting board and let cool for about 15 minutes (or until you can comfortably handle it). Slice or shred into small strips. Return the meat to the liquid.

4. Serve hot.

SERVING TIP: Like many salted Korean side dishes, this braised beef will stay good for a couple weeks if stored in an airtight container in the refrigerator. Because it is very salty, it is usually eaten in small amounts with rice and other dishes.

Chapter Seven

SOUPS AND STEWS

Traditional Korean meals include a bowl of soup or stew for each person, and sometimes the stew serves as the main dish and is set in the middle of the table to be shared family-style. Because Korean meals don't have courses, soup is not an appetizer or first course; you enjoy it with all the other dishes at the table.

Because there is so much variety in flavors and textures at a Korean meal, you should try to coordinate your soup or stew with the rest of the dishes. For example, soups with a clear broth go well with mixed rice dishes (bibimbap), and creamy, soybean-paste soups go well with grilled or braised dishes.

SOFT TOFU STEW

순두부찌개 *sundubu jjigae*

Sundubu jjigae is a steaming, spicy tofu stew that can be made in a variety of ways. Many Korean restaurants make their sundubu with pork and kimchi, and it's a delicious combination. When I make this dish at home, I prefer to make it with kimchi and eggs or with seafood like clams with an anchovy base. Other popular variations include beef, shrimp, and mushrooms. In restaurants, sundubu jjigae is served bubbling hot in traditional earthenware bowls. Raw egg is folded into the stew and cooks from the heat of the stew. *Serves 4*

PREP TIME: 5 MINUTES / COOK TIME: 30 MINUTES

Vegetarian-Friendly

2 tablespoons toasted sesame oil

½ pound (about 1 cup) thinly sliced beef or pork

½ tablespoon finely chopped garlic

2 tablespoons gochugaru

2 cups Anchovy Stock (page 46), Beef Stock (page 47), vegetarian stock, or water

2 tablespoons soy sauce

3 cups soft tofu, cubed

1 pound live clams or 1 cup shucked clams, rinsed

2 scallions, sliced

Eggs (optional)

COOKING TIP: This tofu stew can be made mild to very spicy. This recipe is what I'd consider to be standard (medium hot), but you can omit the gochugaru and the gochujang for a nonspicy version.

1. In a stockpot, warm the sesame oil over medium-high heat. Add the beef, garlic, and gochugaru and stir-fry for about 5 minutes.

2. Add the stock and soy sauce to the pot, stir, and bring to a simmer. Add the tofu and return to simmer.

3. Reduce the heat to medium-low, add the clams, and simmer, uncovered, about 10 minutes, until the shells of live clams open or the shucked clams shrink. Discard any clams that did not open.

4. Stir in the scallions and remove the pot from the heat.

5. Crack 1 or 2 eggs, if using, into the pot about 2 minutes before you turn off the heat.

INGREDIENT TIP: Uncoagulated tofu (pressed, with less water) is sold in tubes, but you can use silken tofu if you can't find the really soft kind.

KIMCHI STEW

This spicy Kimchi Stew (*kimchi jjigae* or *kimchichigae*) is a classic Korean dish
that is almost miraculous in how it can transform leftover or older kimchi.
Fiery hot, hearty, and full of flavor, the dish is perfect for cold winter days,
but Koreans eat it anytime, anywhere. There is a lot of room for variation in
this dish, and everyone has their favorite recipe. Some even use canned tuna.
My favorite additions include potatoes, zucchini, and mushrooms. *Serves 4*

PREP TIME: 10 MINUTES / COOK TIME: 40 MINUTES

Vegetarian-Friendly

¾ pound beef or pork, thinly sliced

1 tablespoon toasted sesame oil, divided

2 cups Napa Cabbage Kimchi
(page 54), roughly chopped

½ sweet onion, chopped

2 garlic cloves, finely chopped

1 tablespoon gochujang

1 tablespoon gochugaru

1 tablespoon soy sauce

3 cups water

½ (12- to 14-ounce) block firm tofu, cubed

2 scallions, chopped

1. If using beef, sauté the meat in ½ table-spoon of the sesame oil in a stockpot for
2 to 3 minutes over medium-high heat. If
using pork, you can halve or omit the oil.

2. Add the kimchi and stir-fry for about
5 minutes.

3. Add the remaining ½ tablespoon
sesame oil, the onion, garlic, gochujang,
gochugaru, and soy sauce and stir to
combine. Add the water, stir, and bring
to a boil. Reduce the heat to medium and
simmer for 15 minutes. Then add the tofu
and simmer for 15 more minutes.

4. Serve hot, sprinkled with the scallions.

SUBSTITUTION TIP: If you want to make a
vegetarian version, just omit the meat and
use vegetable stock instead of water.

INGREDIENT TIP: If using beef, tenderloin
is best, but you can use tougher cuts like
stew beef and simmer the stew longer.
If using pork, then bacon, pork belly, or
SPAM work well. If using canned tuna,
add it in step 3.

RICE CAKE SOUP

떡국 *tteok guk*

This soup, filled with soft, thinly sliced rice cakes (tteok), is always eaten on New Year's Day in Korea. Soothing and simple, it takes less than 30 minutes to cook, if you use premade or store-bought broth. It's also common to add dumplings and/or sliced beef to the soup for a heartier dish. This recipe calls for soup soy sauce, which is soy sauce that is a lighter in color but saltier than regular soy sauce. You can find it at Korean grocery stores or other Asian venues as well as online. *Serves 4*

PREP TIME: 20 MINUTES / COOK TIME: 10 MINUTES

Vegetarian-Friendly

1 (1-pound) package Korean flat oval rice cakes

6 cups Anchovy Stock (page 46), Beef Stock (page 47), or chicken broth (if using store-bought broth, see Substitution Tip following)

Soup soy sauce

1 teaspoon freshly ground black pepper

2 eggs, beaten

1 sheet dried seaweed, cut into thin slices

2 scallions, chopped, for garnish (optional)

SUBSTITUTION TIP: If you are using store-bought broth and it is not low-sodium, then mix 4 cups broth with 2 cups water.

SUBSTITUTION TIP: For a vegetarian version, use vegetable broth.

1. Soak the rice cakes in cold water for about 20 minutes. Drain.

2. In a medium stockpot over medium-high heat, add the stock and bring it to a boil. Season with soup soy sauce and the pepper, and stir.

3. Reduce the heat to medium-low, add the rice cakes, and simmer until tender, about 10 minutes.

4. While soup is cooking, cook the eggs into a thin, flat omelet. Cut the omelet into thin slices.

5. To serve, ladle the soup into 4 individual bowls and garnish with the egg strips, seaweed strips, and scallions (if using).

COOKING TIP: If you don't want to soak the rice cakes beforehand, you don't have to. You will need to add 6 to 8 minutes of cooking time, and your broth will be thicker.

INGREDIENT TIP: Common additions to this dish include beef strips and dumplings.

SEAWEED SOUP

미역국 *miyeok guk*

This soup is known as the "birthday soup" in Korea, because it's given to postpartum mothers recovering from childbirth. As a reminder, it's served and eaten as part of birthday meals. It's naturally low in calories and fat and high in calcium, iodine, and other vitamins and minerals, so it's a light and healthy soup that's good anytime. *Serves 4*

PREP TIME: 35 MINUTES / COOK TIME: 55 MINUTES

Vegetarian-Friendly, Vegan-Friendly

1 ounce dried seaweed (wakame or sea mustard)

1 tablespoon toasted sesame oil

2 garlic cloves, finely chopped

2 tablespoons soup soy sauce

2 cups Anchovy Stock (page 46), Beef Stock (page 47), or vegetable broth

1 cup water

Salt

INGREDIENT TIP: Wakame or sea mustard is a dried sea plant that looks like it's tangled, unlike the roasted seaweed sheets used for making kimbap or sushi rolls. The 1 ounce required in the recipe looks very small, but after rehydrating, it is about 2 cups.

1. In a large bowl, cover the seaweed with water and soak for 30 minutes.

2. Drain the seaweed, squeeze out excess water, and cut into 2-inch pieces with kitchen shears.

3. In a stockpot over medium heat, add the sesame oil and sauté the seaweed for 2 minutes.

4. Add the garlic and soup soy sauce and sauté for another 2 minutes.

5. Add the stock and the water to the pot, stir it in, and raise the heat to high. When the soup begins to boil, reduce the heat to low and simmer for 20 minutes, or until the soup looks a little milky.

6. Serve immediately.

COOKING TIP: This is the simplest way to make Korean seaweed soup and how I generally make it. If you are making this soup for a special occasion (like a birthday), you can add chicken, beef, or clams.

SOYBEAN PASTE STEW

된장찌개 *doenjang jjigae*

This thick, fragrant stew (*doenjang jjigae*) is a Korean comfort food that is especially popular in the cold winter months. Korean bean paste (*doenjang*) is made out of fermented soybeans, so it's similar to Japanese miso paste but is bolder and more powerful. Doenjang jjigae is wonderfully hearty and can be made with almost any vegetables you have on hand. The common way to make this dish is with zucchini, potato, and chiles, but it's delicious with carrots, any squash, and turnips as well. *Serves 4*

PREP TIME: 10 MINUTES / COOK TIME: 30 MINUTES

Vegetarian-Friendly

6 ounces beef or shrimp, peeled
   and deveined, sliced

1 teaspoon vegetable oil

3 cups Anchovy Stock (page 46), Beef Stock
   (page 47), or packaged low-sodium stock

½ onion, chopped

1 teaspoon finely chopped garlic

½ zucchini, cut in half lengthwise and sliced

1 small potato, cut into large dice

1 Korean green chile, seeded and thinly sliced

3 tablespoons doenjang

2 teaspoons gochujang

1 teaspoon gochugaru

1 (12- to 14-ounce) block
   firm tofu, cut into large dice

1 scallion, chopped

1. If using beef, add the vegetable oil to a nonstick stockpot over high heat, and sauté the beef until slightly browned. If using shrimp, skip this step and just add the shrimp with the vegetables.

2. Add the anchovy stock, onion, garlic, zucchini, potato, and chile, stir to combine, and bring to a boil.

3. Reduce the heat to medium and add the doenjang, gochujang, gochugaru, and tofu. Stir gently to combine. When the stew begins to boil again, turn off heat.

4. Serve hot, sprinkled with the scallions.

SUBSTITUTION TIP: If you don't have home-made or packaged stock, you can use water to make this stew, but increase the amount of soybean paste you use and season with salt toward the end of cooking time.

SUBSTITUTION TIP: To make a vegetarian version of this stew, use vegetable broth and omit any meat or seafood.

SOYBEAN SPROUT SOUP

콩나물국 *kong namulguk*

Korean bean sprout soup is a clear, light soup with a refreshing flavor. It's incredibly easy to cook and costs almost nothing to make, so it's a staple for all seasons. It is a popular hangover remedy, because of the vitamins and nutrients in bean sprouts. Add a splash of gochugaru and it's a good tonic for colds as well. *Serves 4*

PREP TIME: 10 MINUTES / COOK TIME: 45 MINUTES

Vegetarian-Friendly, Vegan-Friendly

2 garlic cloves, minced

1 tablespoon toasted sesame oil

6 cups water, Anchovy Stock (page 46), or vegetable stock

2 tablespoons soy sauce

3 cups soybean sprouts, washed, and roots trimmed if desired

1 teaspoon salt

1 tablespoon gochugaru (optional)

2 scallions or chives, chopped (optional)

1. In a medium stockpot over medium heat, sauté the garlic in the sesame oil for 2 to 3 minutes.

2. Add the water (or stock), soy sauce, bean sprouts, and salt, and bring to a boil over high heat. Reduce the heat to low and simmer for 25 to 30 minutes, or until you can smell the strong odor of bean sprouts cooking. Skim the foam off the top while it's cooking.

3. If you're making the spicy version, add the gochugaru 5 minutes before turning off the heat.

4. If you're using scallions or chives, add them to the pot at the end and then immediately take off the heat.

5. Serve hot.

SUBSTITUTION TIP: This is a perfect soup to serve as a side dish because it's so light, but you can make it heartier with beef or tofu.

TOFU HOT POT

두부전골 *dubu jeongol*

This colorful hot pot is a modern version of a traditional Korean royal court dish. This kind of cuisine, which has recently experienced a revival because of the popularity of historical Korean dramas, was the food of the royal court during the Chosun Dynasty (1392 to 1910). The food is more subtle and delicate than everyday Korean cooking, and presentation is particularly important. This recipe is a modern version of an old dish, so it doesn't require elaborate preparation. *Jeongol* is usually made in a large shallow pot and cooked right at the table. If you don't have a small portable stove, you can also just make this on the stove and serve it at the table family style. *Serves 3*

PREP TIME: 15 MINUTES / COOK TIME: 10 MINUTES

Vegetarian-Friendly, Vegan-Friendly

10 ounces assorted mushrooms (shiitake, oyster, crimini, or enoki)

2 scallions, cut into large strips

2 ounces watercress, cut into 2-inch pieces

1 (12- to 14-ounce) block tofu, halved and sliced into thin rectangles

1 tablespoon soup soy sauce, plus more for seasoning

2½ cups vegetable stock

Salt

Freshly ground black pepper

1. Cut the mushrooms into large strips.

2. Arrange the mushrooms, scallions, watercress, and tofu neatly in sections around a shallow pot.

3. Add the soup soy sauce and stock and bring to a boil over medium-high heat. Simmer for 5 minutes.

4. Taste the broth and season with additional soy sauce, salt, and pepper, if needed.

VARIATION TIP: You can add other vegetables like radishes, Napa cabbage, zucchini, and carrots to the hot pot. For a contemporary spin that is decidedly unroyal, add some dumplings and uncooked ramen noodles to the pot.

SPINACH AND CLAM SOUP

조개 시금치국 *jogae sigeumchiguk*

Spinach and clam soup is a delicious, flavorful, healthy side dish
for any Korean meal. The recipe is simple and it takes less than
30 minutes to make, but it tastes awesome. Make sure all the fresh
clams are tightly closed, and discard any that are open before cooking.
Anchovy powder is made from dried anchovies and can be found in
Korean grocery stores, other Asian grocers, and online. *Serves 4*

PREP TIME: 15 MINUTES / COOK TIME: 15 MINUTES

Gluten-Free

1 pound fresh spinach, with thick stems
    trimmed and coarsely chopped

5 cups water

¼ cup doenjang or gluten-free doenjang

1 teaspoon anchovy powder
    (*myulchi karu or myeolchi garu*)

2 tablespoons minced garlic

4 scallions, chopped

20 littleneck clams (fewer if you are using
    large clams), rinsed and scrubbed

SUBSTITUTION TIP: If you don't have or can't
find anchovy powder, then you can use
a traditional anchovy broth instead of the
water. If you can't find the ingredients
for that broth either, you can substitute
chicken, beef, or vegetable broth.

1. Blanch the spinach for 30 seconds in
boiling water, and drain.

2. Put the 5 cups of water into large stockpot over high heat.

3. Add the doenjang gradually, stirring and using a whisk to dissolve,
if necessary.

4. Stir in the anchovy powder, garlic, and
scallions, and bring the broth to a boil.

5. Reduce the heat to medium-high, add
the spinach and clams, and cook for 5 to
10 minutes, until the clams open. Discard
any clams that did not open.

6. Serve immediately.

SUBSTITUTION TIP: You can use miso paste
(fermented soybean paste) instead of
doenjang in this soup, substitute beef for
the clams, or use kale or Swiss chard in
place of the spinach.

SEAFOOD SOUP
WITH RAMEN NOODLES

짬뽕 *jjamppong*

A soothing mix of noodles, seafood, vegetables, and meat in a spicy, savory soup, *jjamppong* (or *champong*) is one of the most popular Chinese-Korean dishes made and enjoyed all over Korea.

The word jjampong comes from the Japanese word for "mix," and the dish itself was supposedly created by Chinese immigrants living in Nagasaki, Japan. It's easy to make and change up with ingredients you have on hand. At most restaurants, you'll see squid, shrimp, and mussels with vegetables and egg or wheat noodles in a fiery red soup base. This recipe uses instant ramen noodles for a richer, more contemporary variation. *Serves 3*

PREP TIME: 15 MINUTES, PLUS 1 HOUR FOR SOAKING / COOK TIME: 15 MINUTES

Vegetarian-Friendly

4 dried shiitake mushrooms, soaked and thinly sliced

6 mussels or clams, scrubbed clean

1 tablespoon vegetable oil

2 teaspoons minced garlic

1 teaspoon minced fresh peeled ginger

1 tablespoon gochugaru

⅓ cup pork, thinly sliced

1 small sweet onion, halved and sliced

½ medium carrot, julienned

1 scallion, cut into 2-inch pieces

1 cup napa cabbage, sliced into 1-inch chunks (or substitute bok choy or thinly sliced American green cabbage)

1 package uncooked ramen noodles

7 cups Anchovy Stock (page 46), Beef Stock (page 47), or chicken stock

6 medium shrimp, peeled and deveined

½ cup squid, cleaned and thinly sliced

1 green chile, like Korean or jalapeño, seeded and sliced

1 red chile, like Korean or Spanish, seeded and sliced

2 tablespoons soy sauce

1 teaspoon fish sauce (optional)

Salt

Freshly ground black pepper

1. In a small bowl of room temperature water, soak the mushrooms for one hour.

2. In a stockpot, bring the mussels and 2 cups of water to a boil over high heat. Cover, reduce the heat to low, and simmer for 5 to 10 minutes until the shells open. Discard any mussels that did not open. Set aside the mussels, and reserve 1 cup of the mussel cooking liquid and discard the rest.

3. Heat the vegetable oil in a deep large skillet or large wok over medium-high heat. Add the garlic and ginger and stir-fry for about 1 minute.

4. Add the gochugaru, pork, and onion, and stir-fry for about 2 minutes.

5. Add the carrots and scallion and stir-fry for about 3 minutes. Add the cabbage, ramen noodles, and stock (including the 1 cup reserved cooking liquid) and bring to a boil. Reduce the heat to medium and let simmer for 5 minutes.

6. Add the shrimp and squid and cook for about 1 minute.

7. Add the cooked mussels and mix everything together gently.

8. Gently stir in the soaked and sliced mushrooms, green chile, red chile, soy sauce, and fish sauce (if using), and season with salt and pepper.

9. With a slotted spoon, scoop the ramen noodles into 3 individual soup bowls, and ladle the soup over the top.

10. Serve immediately.

SERVING TIP: Korean-style Chinese restaurants in Korea usually serve this dish with slices of pickled radish.

SUBSTITUTION TIP: To make a vegetarian version of this Korean-Chinese dish, use vegetable broth instead of the anchovy stock and double the amount of mushrooms in this dish. You can also use a variety of other mushrooms to go with the shiitake mushrooms.

COOKING TIP: At many Korean restaurants, the seafood is simmered for a long time along with the rest of the ingredients, but I feel like that can make it tough by the time it's served.

SPICY COD STEW

매운탕 *maeuntang*

This Korean fish stew is a little bit spicy and sweet and has dozens of different variations. Cod (*daegu*) is my favorite fish to use, but you can also use red snapper, halibut, yellow croaker, corvina, sea bass, or pollock and get a delicious stew. Buy a whole fish and have it cleaned and filleted, saving the fish head for broth. In some Korean restaurants, you can choose your fish while it's still swimming in the tank. The chefs at the restaurant will prepare some sashimi (*hwe*) for you, and then they will make this soup from the leftover parts of the fish (the head, leftover flesh, and bones) for you to enjoy after your raw fish course. In Korean, *maeun* means spicy and *tang* means soup or stew. *Serves 4*

PREP TIME: 10 MINUTES / COOK TIME: 30 MINUTES

Gluten-Free

1 whole cod, filleted and the head separated

8 ounces Korean white radish or daikon, peeled and cut into 1-inch pieces

2 garlic cloves, chopped

1 red Korean chile (or Spanish), halved and seeded

1 green Korean chile, halved and seeded

½ sweet onion, sliced into strips

1 tablespoon gochugaru

3 tablespoons gochujang or gluten-free gochujang

1 tablespoon soy sauce or gluten-free soy sauce

2 scallions, cut into 1-inch pieces

Salt

Freshly ground black pepper

½ (12- or 14-ounce) block firm tofu, cut into large cubes

4 ounces edible chrysanthemum leaves

½ zucchini, halved lengthwise and sliced

1. Cut the cod into several pieces.

2. In a medium pot over medium-high heat, bring 3½ cups water and the fish head to a boil. Reduce the heat to medium and add the radish, garlic, red chile, green chile, onion, gochugaru, gochujang, and soy sauce. Cook for 5 to 6 minutes. Don't stir too much while the stew is cooking to keep the broth clear.

3. Season the broth with salt and pepper.

4. Remove the fish head and discard. Add the fish pieces to the broth and simmer until the fish is tender, 3 to 4 minutes.

5. Add the scallions, tofu, chrysanthemum leaves, and zucchini and simmer for 2 to 3 minutes more. Do not stir anymore after this point. Season with salt and pepper.

INGREDIENT TIP: For vegetable variations, you can include soybean sprouts, pumpkin, mushrooms, scallions, watercress, or Korean parsley (*minari* or water dropwort). Some cooks and restaurants also add clams, oysters, or other shellfish. Radish, zucchini, and chiles are the essentials for me if I'm making this at home.

SUBSTITION TIP: If you can't find chrysanthemum leaves, you can substitute watercress or even spinach.

STUFFED CHICKEN SOUP WITH GINGSENG

삼계탕 *samgyetang*

Samgyetang is a fragrant, gorgeous soup that is surprisingly easy to make. Just like chicken soup is a Western cold remedy and wintertime food, this soup is also a Korean restorative. But it's more traditionally eaten and enjoyed during the summer months, as Koreans like to drink hot soup or stews in warm weather in an effort to fight the heat with heat. The theory behind this practice is that your body is better able to regulate itself and stay cool in the summer heat after being detoxed and rejuvenated by a bowl of samgyetang. Because of the medicinal properties of ginseng, some Korean mothers give this soup to their newlywed children. Dried red dates may be labeled in the grocery store as jujubes, Chinese dates, or Korean dates. *Serves 6*

PREP TIME: 10 MINUTES / COOK TIME: 2 HOURS

Gluten-Free

2 small whole chickens or Cornish game hens

½ cup Korean sticky rice (*chapsal*), washed and drained

7 to 8 chestnuts, peeled

8 garlic cloves, peeled

2 roots dried ginseng

8 to 10 dried red dates, rinsed

¼-inch piece peeled ginger, cut in half

9 cups water

Salt

Freshly ground black pepper

2 scallions, chopped, for garnish

INGREDIENT TIP: At the grocery story, the sweet rice might be labeled "chapsal" or "glutinous rice."

1. Remove innards from the chickens and rinse, inside and out.

2. Trim off any visible fat, but don't trim any skin.

3. Stuff the rice, chestnuts, and garlic into the body cavities. Use toothpicks if necessary to keep the stuffing inside.

4. Put the stuffed birds in a large stockpot and add the ginseng roots, dates, and ginger. Pour the water over the top. Bring to a boil over high heat, and then reduce the heat to low. Cover and simmer until the thigh bones pull away easily, 1 to 1½ hours. Don't cook so long that the birds begin to come apart. They should stay intact.

5. During cooking, occasionally skim the fat and foam from the surface of the water.

6. Season with salt and pepper. Serve in individual bowls and garnish with the scallions.

HANGOVER SOUP

해장국 *haejangguk*

Haejangguk translates as "hangover soup," and there are many different Korean soups that could carry this name. Two of the most common hangover soups in Korea are pork bone and ox blood soup and dried pollock soup. This kimchi and bean-sprout version is my favorite, though, and it seems there is some scientific evidence to support the hangover remedy claim. All of the Korean hangover soups are restorative because they replenish vitamins, minerals, and sodium, but the bean sprouts in this soup have asparagine, which is the main ingredient in some over-the-counter hangover pills. *Serves 4*

PREP TIME: 15 MINUTES / COOK TIME: 20 MINUTES

Vegetarian-Friendly

½ tablespoon toasted sesame oil

¼ cup sliced beef

2 tablespoons minced garlic

1 tablespoon soup soy sauce

¼ cup kimchi, rinsed, drained, and chopped

3 cups Anchovy Stock (page 46)
    or vegetable stock

1 cup bean sprouts

1 cup chopped kale

2 teaspoons gochugaru

2 teaspoons sesame seeds

½ cup chopped scallions, for garnish

1. In a stockpot, warm the sesame oil over medium-high heat. Add the beef and garlic and sauté for about 3 minutes.

2. Add the soup soy sauce, kimchi, and anchovy stock and bring to a boil.

3. Add the bean sprouts, kale, and gochugaru. Cover and simmer for about 15 minutes.

4. Add the sesame seeds and cook for 1 more minute.

5. Serve the soup ladled into 4 individual bowls and garnished with chopped scallions.

SUBSTITUTION TIP: For a vegetarian version, use vegetable stock and omit the beef and sesame oil.

FEAST CHICKEN NOODLE SOUP

잔치국수 *janchi guksu*

This chicken noodle soup is often served at wedding feasts, important birthday celebrations, and banquets. The name *janchi* means feast in Korean and *guksu* means noodles. Because noodles represent long life in Korea, this is a symbolic dish for honored guests. Despite traditionally being a special-occasion dish, this is an easy soup to make and enjoy at home. *Serves 6 to 8*

PREP TIME: 10 MINUTES / COOK TIME: 60 MINUTES

1 small chicken, rinsed inside and out

8 garlic cloves

2 leeks, white and light green parts, trimmed and cut in half

15 peppercorns

1 package somyun noodles (*somen* or *somyeon*, which are thin wheat noodles), cooked according to package directions

1 zucchini

1 carrot

1 teaspoon vegetable oil

2 eggs, whites and yolks separated into two small bowls, lightly beaten

Salt

Freshly ground black pepper

Toasted sesame oil, for garnish

1. Put the chicken in a stockpot and add water to just cover. Add the garlic, leeks, and peppercorns and bring to a boil over high heat. Reduce the heat to low and simmer for about 40 minutes, or until the chicken is tender.

2. While the chicken is cooking, cook the noodles according to the package directions. Drain, cover to keep warm, and set aside.

3. Slice the zucchini and carrot into thin strips.

4. In a medium skillet over medium-high heat, warm the vegetable oil. Add the zucchini and carrot in a skillet and sauté for 2 to 3 minutes. Set aside.

5. In a medium nonstick skillet over medium-high heat, fry the egg whites into a very thin, flat omelet, about 1 minute per side. Transfer to a cutting board.

6. Wipe out the nonstick skillet if it needs it, and then fry the beaten egg yolks over medium-high heat into a very thin, flat omelet, about 1 minute per side. Transfer to the cutting board.

7. Slice the omelets into thin strips, about the same size as the vegetables. Set aside.

8. Transfer the cooked chicken to a cutting board. Separate the meat from the bones, discarding the bones, fat, and skin. Shred the chicken into small strips. Season lightly with salt and pepper.

9. Strain the broth, discard the solids, and season with salt and pepper. Return the broth to the stove to reheat at high heat, if not still hot.

10. To serve, place the cooked noodles in a large soup bowl and top with the seasoned chicken meat, vegetables, and eggs. Ladle the broth into the bowl and finish with a drizzle of sesame oil.

SERVING TIP: Serve the soup with Sweet and Spicy Dipping Sauce (page 50) on the side.

SHORT RIB SOUP

갈비탕 *galbitang*

Galbitang is a rich, hearty soup made from beef short ribs, Korean radish, and glass noodles (made from sweet potatoes). It's a soup that needs to simmer for a long time, but it is still easy to make with very little hands-on time. Some people like to add some chile seasoning at the table to give it an extra kick, and you can experiment with adding some chile-garlic sauce if you want a spicier version. English-cut short ribs are cut parallel with the bone, with one bone per piece. *4 servings*

PREP TIME: 1 HOUR / COOK TIME: 90 MINUTES

Gluten-Free

2 pounds English-cut beef short ribs, cut into 2-inch squares

3 tablespoons soy sauce or gluten-free soy sauce

2 teaspoons toasted sesame oil

6 garlic cloves, 4 cloves sliced and 2 cloves minced

1 teaspoon freshly and finely ground black pepper

½ large Korean radish or 2 daikon radishes, peeled and cut into 1-inch slices

2 teaspoons salt

4 ounces glass noodles

2 scallions, cut into 1-inch pieces

Gochugaru, for garnish (optional)

1. Rinse the ribs well with cold water to remove any dried blood or bones. Soak the ribs in cold water for 1 hour. This helps draw some blood out. Drain and discard the water.

2. While soaking the meat, make the seasoning sauce. In a medium bowl, stir together the soy sauce, sesame oil, minced and sliced garlic, and pepper, and then add the radish and toss to mix well.

3. Put the meat in a stockpot over high heat and cover with water. Bring to a boil and simmer vigorously for 5 minutes. Remove the meat from the pot with a slotted spoon. Discard the water and rinse the pot.

4. Return the meat to the same pot and cover with 4 cups fresh water. Bring to a boil, and simmer over high heat for 30 minutes.

5. Add the seasoning sauce–radish mixture and the salt, stir, and cook for an additional 10 minutes.

6. Add the noodles and cook for another 4 minutes.

7. Add the scallions and cook for another 1 minute.

8. Serve hot, garnished with gochugaru (if desired).

COOKING TIP: Many Korean cookbooks call for soaking ribs and meat in water for a couple of hours before cooking in addition to blanching the meat before boiling. Blanching the meat will always give a clearer soup and reduces the amount of fat and foam you need to skim off. There are times when the water remains very clear after the meat has soaked and times when it does look pink, so I'm guessing that the extensive soaking and blanching is probably an old tradition before most of us bought our meat drained and shrink-wrapped in plastic at the grocery store.

BEEF OXTAIL SOUP

꼬리곰탕 *kkori gomtang*

This rich, comforting soup is milky white from long simmering. It has only a few ingredients so it's easy to make, but it does require a lot of slow cooking. Some people simmer their soup for many hours to get the best tasting soup, or *tang*. Oxtails are bones from the tail of steers. Serve with rice and additional salt and pepper, if you wish, so that each person can add the amount of rice and seasoning they wish. Also serve with kimchi on the side. *Serves 5*

PREP TIME: 5 MINUTES, PLUS 1 HOUR FOR SOAKING / COOK TIME: 4 HOURS 30 MINUTES

Gluten-Free

3 pounds oxtails, trimmed of visible fat

1 tablespoon salt

4 garlic cloves

10 to 12 peppercorns

4 scallions, chopped

Freshly ground black pepper

TIP: This recipe makes a large amount, so after you chill your *gomtang* in the refrigerator, any residual fat will solidify on the top of the soup. Discard the solid fat before reheating the soup.

VARIATION TIP: You can serve this soup with rice cakes or sweet potato noodles in addition to the rice.

1. Soak the oxtails in cold water for 1 hour. Drain and rinse.

2. In a large stockpot, cover the oxtails with about 15 cups of water and bring to a boil over high heat, for 10 minutes, regularly skimming any fat or foam from the surface. Reduce the heat to medium and simmer for about 30 minutes, continuing to skim the foam. Then lower the heat to low and simmer gently for about 3 hours.

3. Transfer the oxtails to a plate and set aside.

4. Using a fine-meshed strainer, strain any floating pieces and fat from the soup. Return the soup to the stockpot.

5. Reduce the heat to low and bring the soup to a simmer. Add the salt, garlic, and peppercorns to the pot. Continue to simmer for about 30 minutes. Discard the peppercorns and garlic.

6. To serve, put the oxtails in individual large soup bowls and ladle the broth over the top. Sprinkle with the chopped scallions and season with black pepper.

SPICY BEEF STEW

육개장 *yukgaejang*

Yukgaejang is a spicy, hearty Korean stew that warms you from your lips to your toes. Full of meat and vegetables, this stew is fiery red, bold, and spicy. It is a one-pot meal that requires very little hands-on time but tastes like you've spent all day making it. *Serves 6*

PREP TIME: 15 MINUTES / COOK TIME: 90 MINUTES

🍴🍴🍴

Gluten-Free

1 pound beef brisket, trimmed

8 scallions, cut into thirds

1 cup bean sprouts

¾ cup dried presoaked fernbrake (*gosari* or bracken fern fiddleheads), rinsed

2 tablespoons minced garlic

2 tablespoons toasted sesame oil

2 teaspoons gochugaru

2 tablespoons gochujang or gluten-free gochujang

2 teaspoons soy sauce or gluten-free soy sauce

1 teaspoon freshly ground black pepper

2 eggs, lightly beaten

1 cup cooked glass noodles (optional)

SERVING TIP: This soup is used as both a cold remedy and a hangover remedy. It definitely warms you from the inside and clears your sinuses, so I like to eat it when I'm feeling under the weather.

1. In a large stockpot over high heat, bring the brisket and about 4 quarts of water to a boil.

2. Immediately reduce the heat to low and simmer until the meat is tender, about 1 hour, skimming off the fat and foam that appear on the surface of the broth during cooking.

3. Remove the meat from the broth, leaving the broth in the pot.

4. When the meat is cool enough to handle, shred it along the grain with your hands or two forks.

5. In a large bowl, combine the shredded beef with the scallions, bean sprouts, and gosari (fernbrake).

6. Add the garlic, sesame oil, gochugaru, gochujang, soy sauce, and pepper.

7. Add the meat mixture to the broth in the pot and bring to a boil. Reduce the heat to medium-low and simmer for about 5 minutes. Taste and add additional soy sauce, if needed.

8. Swirl the beaten egg into the soup, stirring. Add the noodles (if using).

9. Serve immediately.

Chapter Eight

RICE AND NOODLES

Rice is the staple food of the Korean table. *Bap*, which means rice in Korean, is also used interchangeably with the word for meal. Although Western-style breakfasts of toast and eggs are now popular in Korea, traditionally Koreans ate rice with every meal of the day.

Koreans have made and eaten noodles for thousands of years, and they are stir-fried, served cold, or used in soups, stews, and salads. Korean noodles are usually made out of buckwheat, wheat flour, or sweet potato starch. Noodles represent long life in Korea, so they are a popular part of birthday meals.

COLD BUCKWHEAT NOODLES

냉면 *naengmyeon*

Naengmyeon (or *naengmyun*) is a Korean cold noodle dish made of thin, slightly chewy buckwheat noodles topped with egg, meat, vegetables, and a savory, vinegary ice-cold broth. This dish originated in the North Korean mountains as a wintertime meal. Because buckwheat grows well in high altitudes, these noodles were an important staple for Koreans living in harsh winter climates. *Serves 2*

PREP TIME: 10 MINUTES, PLUS 30 MINUTES FOR CHILLING / COOK TIME: 10 MINUTES

2 cups chicken broth

2 cups low-sodium beef broth

1 tablespoon brown rice vinegar

2 tablespoons white vinegar

¼ pound buckwheat noodles (*naengmyeon*)

Ice cubes, for serving

1 hard-boiled egg, halved

1 small Asian pear, julienned or cut into paper-thin slices

½ kirby or pickling cucumber, seeded and julienned or cut into paper-thin slices

¼ cup pickled radish

½ cup cooked beef brisket or cooked chicken, sliced

Vinegar, sugar, and Korean mustard, for serving

INGREDIENT TIP: Naengmyeon noodles are thin noodles made from buckwheat and sweet potato, but make sure you're not buying soba or *memil guksu*.

1. In a large bowl, mix the chicken broth, beef broth, rice vinegar, and white vinegar. Chill in the refrigerator for at least 30 minutes.

2. Cook the noodles according to the package directions. Drain and rinse well in cold water.

3. Distribute the noodles in 2 serving bowls, mounding them at the bottom. Cut the noodle mounds in a few places with kitchen shears after plating.

4. Pour a generous amount of the chilled broth mixture over the noodles to almost cover them, and add a few ice cubes.

5. Place half a boiled egg, the pear, cucumber slices, pickled radish, and beef brisket slices on top of the noodles.

6. Serve immediately, with vinegar, sugar, and Korean mustard to pass at the table.

SUBSTITUTION TIP: If you can't get Asian pear, you can use Bosc pear. If you can't get any pears, use a crisp apple like Fuji.

SPICY COLD NOODLES

비빔국수 *bibim guksu*

This spicy cold noodle dish is a great basic recipe that can be made in dozens of variations once you master the sauce. Just like with other Korean dishes, you can use this recipe as a base for experimenting. If you are craving meat, add some chicken or sliced meat as a topping. If you want to make this a salad-noodle dish, feel free to add chopped spinach, kale, or cabbage to the mix. The thin wheat flour noodles are called *somen* in Japanese and *somyeon* in Korean. *Serves 2*

PREP TIME: 10 MINUTES / COOK TIME: 10 MINUTES

Vegetarian-Friendly

4 bundles thin wheat flour noodles (*somyeon*), cooked according to package directions

3 tablespoons gochujang

½ tablespoon rice vinegar

2 teaspoons honey

2 garlic cloves, minced

1 tablespoon soy sauce

½ tablespoon gochugaru

1 tablespoon toasted sesame oil

½ tablespoon sesame seeds

¼ cup chopped lettuce, for garnish

1 cucumber, seeded and cut into matchsticks, for garnish

1 hard-boiled egg, quartered lengthwise, for garnish

2 scallions, chopped, for garnish (optional)

1. Rinse the cooked noodles in cold water to stop the cooking. Drain them well in a colander and shake out any water. Set aside.

2. To make the sauce, in a small bowl, stir together the gochujang, vinegar, honey, garlic, soy sauce, gochugaru, sesame oil, and sesame seeds. Mix well.

3. In a large bowl, mix the sauce mixture with the cold noodles, tossing to coat completely.

4. Serve the seasoned noodles in 2 bowls, garnished with lettuce, cucumber, egg, and chopped scallion, if using.

SUBSTITUTION TIP: Thinly sliced apples or Asian pear are a delicious topping for these cold noodles. You can also use the Soy Sauced Potatoes (page 102) as a special topping on this dish.

COLD SOYBEAN NOODLES

콩국수 *kong guksu*

This Korean noodle dish is cold and mild, with a nutty taste that makes it perfect for very hot summer days. It's an easy recipe for even the novice cook, costs almost nothing to make, and is a healthy and filling vegan Korean dish. *Serves 4 to 6*

PREP TIME: 10 MINUTES, PLUS 2 HOURS FOR SOAKING / COOK TIME: 30 MINUTES

Vegetarian-Friendly, Vegan-Friendly

1 cup dried soybeans

8 ounces wheat flour noodles (*somyeon*)

2 teaspoons salt

2 tablespoons toasted sesame seeds

3 tablespoons pine nuts (optional)

3 or 4 ice cubes or ½ cup crushed ice

Matchstick-sliced cucumbers,
    for garnish (optional)

Sliced tomatoes, for garnish (optional)

Additional sesame seeds, pine nuts,
    or peanuts, for garnish (optional)

SERVING TIP: The soybean sauce is basically seasoned soy milk, so you can drink any leftovers if you wish.

1. Soak the soybeans overnight in a bowl of cold water or in hot water for 1 to 2 hours. Drain.

2. Put the soybeans in a medium saucepan and cover with water. Bring to a boil over high heat. Reduce the heat to medium and simmer vigorously for about 20 minutes.

3. Meanwhile, cook the noodles according to the package directions. Rinse them in cold water.

4. Drain the soybeans and rinse them under cold water, rubbing them between your hands to remove the skins.

5. In a blender, purée the cooked soybeans, salt, sesame seeds, and pine nuts, if using, with about 4 cups water. You might have to do this in a few batches. When the mixture becomes smooth, add 3 or 4 ice cubes or ½ cup crushed ice and purée until smooth and frothy. If you want a smoother texture, pass the mixture through a sieve and discard the solids.

6. To serve, put a mound of noodles in each bowl, cover with soybean sauce, and top with any of the garnishes (if desired). You can also add a couple ice cubes to each bowl if you like it very cold.

BEAN SPROUT RICE

콩나물밥 *kong namul bap*

Koreans like to eat rice cooked with different beans and mixed with a variety of vegetables, and *kong namul bap* is a special way to enhance your rice. It's simple and easy to make this in a rice cooker without a lot of fuss. If you're eating this with a lot of other dishes, you may omit the meat. But if you're eating it as a simple meal with just a bowl of soup, then the meat will make your meal more substantial. *Serves 5*

PREP TIME: 5 MINUTES / COOK TIME: 30 MINUTES

Vegetarian-Friendly, Vegan-Friendly

½ cup diced beef or pork, marinated with bulgogi marinade (see recipe for Sliced Barbecued Beef, page 178) (optional)

3 cups uncooked Korean rice

2 cups soybean sprouts

Seasoned Soy Sauce (page 49) or salt

1. Put the meat in the bottom of a rice cooker.

2. Cover the meat with the rice. Add water according to the rice cooker directions. Start the rice cooker.

3. After 5 minutes, if using a pressure rice cooker, or 10 minutes, if using a regular rice cooker, add the soybean sprouts, mixing gently to combine. Let the rice cooker complete its cooking cycle. Once the rice is done, gently fluff the mixture and let sit in the cooker with the lid closed for another 5 minutes before serving.

4. Serve with seasoned soy sauce or salt on the side.

SUBSTITUTION TIP: For a vegetarian version, omit the meat.

VARIATION TIP: This can be a super hearty one-dish meal if you top each bowl with chopped kimchi and a fried egg.

MIXED RICE WITH SASHIMI

회덮밥 *hoedeopbap*

Hoedeopbap combines three foods that Koreans love: raw seafood, rice, and spicy sauces. This is similar to Korean mixed rice (bibimbap), except all of the ingredients are raw and fresh. This big bowl of sushi-grade raw fish, vegetables, and rice comes with a spicy-sweet sauce on the side, so that everyone can add it to suit their own tolerance for spice. I never get tired of making or eating this dish. *Serves 4*

PREP TIME: 15 MINUTES / COOK TIME: 0

Gluten-Free

5 cups cooked rice

2 pounds sushi-grade fish (red snapper, yellowtail, tuna, striped bass, or salmon), cut in ½-inch by 1-inch pieces

1 head red leaf lettuce, chopped

1 small cucumber, thinly sliced

1 small carrot, cut in matchsticks

7 or 8 perilla leaves, thinly sliced

½ Asian pear, peeled, cored, and thinly sliced

1 large sheet roasted laver seaweed, cut in thin strips

Sesame seeds, for garnish (optional)

1 cup seasoned chile paste (*cho gochujang*) or gluten-free gochujang, for serving

1. Divide the rice among 4 bowls.

2. Arrange the fish, lettuce, cucumber, carrot, perilla leaves, and Asian pear neatly on top of the rice. Top with the seaweed strips.

3. If using sesame seeds, sprinkle them over each bowl.

4. Serve with the cho gochujang on the side.

INGREDIENT TIP: Sushi-grade fish is an arbitrary term in the United States, so I recommend that you don't go by the sushi-grade label only, but that you buy any fish you are planning to eat raw from a fishmonger you trust, ideally at a store that sells a lot of fish that will be eaten raw, such as a Japanese or Korean market.

KOREAN-CHINESE NOODLES IN BLACK BEAN SAUCE

자짱면 *jajjangmyeon*

This is one of the most popular takeout dishes in Korea, and it's served at Korean Chinese restaurants. It's a delicious and satisfying comfort food dish that's also inexpensive and easy to make. If you like, use a combination of sweet and white potatoes. *Serves 6 to 8*

PREP TIME: 15 MINUTES / COOK TIME: 25 MINUTES

Vegetarian-Friendly

2 cups diced pork loin

4 medium potatoes, peeled and diced

2 teaspoons vegetable oil

2 medium sweet onions, diced

2 cups black bean paste (*chunjang* or *jajang*)

2 tablespoons toasted sesame oil

2 tablespoons minced garlic

1 tablespoon sugar

6 cups cool water, plus ½ cup

2 large carrots, peeled and cut into large dice

1 medium zucchini, diced

¼ cup cornstarch

3 pounds Chinese flat, thick noodles (dry or fresh) or buckwheat, udon, or linguine noodles

Sliced raw onions, for serving

White vinegar, for serving

COOKING TIP: Although I grew up eating this, I never had it in a Korean restaurant until I was an adult. The restaurant version is usually quite sweet. If you like it that way, add more sugar to the sauce.

1. In a large skillet or wok, sauté the pork and potatoes in the vegetable oil for 2 to 3 minutes over high heat.

2. Add the onions and sauté for 2 to 3 more minutes.

3. Add the bean paste, sesame oil, garlic, and sugar and stir to mix. Sauté for 3 to 4 minutes.

4. Add 6 cups of the water, the carrots, and zucchini, and bring to a boil. Reduce the heat to medium-low.

5. In a small bowl, stir together the cornstarch with the remaining ½ cup water. Add the cornstarch slurry to the pan, stirring, to thicken the sauce. Cook until the vegetables are tender, about 15 minutes.

6. Meanwhile, cook the noodles according to the package directions.

7. To serve, place large mounds of noodles in big soup bowls. Ladle the sauce over the noodles. Place the sliced onions and the vinegar alongside.

MIXED RICE WITH VEGETABLES

비빔밥 *bibimbap*

Bibimbap translates to "mixed rice" in Korean, and it's a colorful one-bowl meal that you can easily tweak for different palates and spice levels. Different regions of Korea have their own versions depending on their local vegetables and taste preferences, so don't feel like you have to stick to the vegetables in this version if you don't like any of the ingredients listed here.

You can also use whatever protein you like in this dish, from beef to chicken to fish. I usually top my bibimbap with an egg fried sunny side-up, but you can make your own version as vegetable or meat-heavy as you wish. *Serves 4*

PREP TIME: 30 MINUTES / COOK TIME: 40 MINUTES

Vegetarian-Friendly, Gluten-Free

For the sauce

3 tablespoons gochujang or gluten-free gochujang

2 tablespoons mirin

1 tablespoon sugar

2 teaspoons sesame seeds

1 teaspoon toasted sesame oil

For the mixed rice

Salt

1 large cucumber, thinly sliced

1½ cups baby spinach, parboiled and squeezed of excess liquid

4 tablespoons plus ½ teaspoon toasted sesame oil, divided

1 tablespoon sesame seeds

1½ cups bean sprouts, parboiled and squeezed of excess liquid

1 medium carrot, cut into matchsticks

4 shiitake mushrooms, thinly sliced

1 medium zucchini, thinly sliced

5 cups cooked rice

4 eggs, fried sunny-side up

2 tablespoons sesame oil, for serving

TO MAKE THE SAUCE

In a small bowl, stir together the gochujang, mirin, sugar, sesame seeds, and sesame oil. Mix well and set aside.

TO MAKE THE MIXED RICE

1. In a medium bowl, prepare a saltwater bath by adding 3 tablespoons of salt to 2 cups of ice water. Immerse the cucumber slices in the bath for 20 minutes and then drain. Squeeze out excess water with your hands.

2. In a small bowl, season the spinach with 2 teaspoons of the sesame oil, 1 teaspoon salt, and a ¼ teaspoon of the sesame seeds. Set aside.

3. In a small bowl, season the bean sprouts with 1½ teaspoons of the sesame oil and 1 teaspoon salt. Set aside.

4. In a medium skillet over medium heat, heat 1 teaspoon of the sesame oil. Add the carrots and a dash of salt, and sauté 1 to 2 minutes, until the carrots are crisp-tender. Remove the carrots and set aside.

5. Add another teaspoon of the sesame oil to the skillet. Add the mushrooms and a dash of salt, and sauté the mushrooms for 1 to 2 minutes until tender. Remove the mushrooms and set aside.

6. Add another teaspoon of the sesame oil to the skillet. Add the zucchini and a dash of salt, and sauté the zucchini for 1 to 2 minutes, until the slices are crisp-tender. Remove the zucchini and set aside.

7. Divide the cooked rice in 4 large bowls and arrange the vegetables on top.

8. Place an egg on top of the vegetables and rice.

9. Garnish each egg with a pinch of sesame seeds.

10. Serve with the sauce and remaining sesame oil.

11. To eat, drizzle the bibimbap sauce and ½ tablespoon sesame oil over the vegetables and egg, and mix everything together with a spoon.

VARIATION TIP: Bibimbap is also tasty when topped with side dishes like Seasoned Radish Strips (see page 91), chopped kimchi (any kimchi variety would do), and shredded Korean roasted laver seaweed (*gim*).

VARIATION TIP: To make *dolsot bibimbap*, spread sesame oil over the inside of large earthenware bowls (see pages 32 to 33 to read about *dolsot* bowls), place the rice inside with vegetables on top, and then heat the bowls on the stove over high heat until the rice begins to make crackling sounds. Top the vegetables with the eggs, remove from the heat, and serve immediately

STIR-FRIED SWEET POTATO NOODLES

잡채 *japchae*

Japchae (or *chapchae*) is one of the most popular noodle dishes in Korea, and also seems to be the one Westerners like best. The foundation of the dish is a mixture of the noodles, soy sauce, garlic, and sesame oil, which goes perfectly with the sweet potato noodles because they absorb so much flavor. *Serves 4*

PREP TIME: 30 MINUTES / COOK TIME: 15 MINUTES

Vegetarian-Friendly

½ pound baby spinach

2 tablespoons vegetable oil

1 tablespoon toasted sesame oil, plus ½ tablespoon

1 sweet onion, sliced into thin strips

2 garlic cloves, finely chopped

2 small carrots, julienned

3 scallions, chopped

½ cup chopped napa cabbage

5 shiitake mushrooms, rehydrated if dried, sliced

8 ounces mung bean noodles or sweet potato noodles (also called cellophane or glass noodles or Chinese vermicelli), cooked according to the package directions

6 ounces beef or pork (optional)

3 tablespoons soy sauce, plus more for seasoning

1 teaspoon sugar

Salt

Sesame seeds, for garnish (optional)

COOKING TIP: The traditional way to make this is to cook all the vegetables separately before adding to the noodles.

1. In a medium saucepan of boiling water, blanch the spinach for about 20 seconds. Drain and gently squeeze with your hands to remove excess water.

2. In a large skillet or wok over medium heat, heat the vegetable oil and 1 tablespoon sesame oil. Add the onion and garlic and stir-fry for about 1 minute.

3. Add the spinach, carrots, scallions, cabbage, and mushrooms and cook until the vegetables are crisp-tender, 4 to 5 minutes.

4. Turn the heat to low, and add the cooked noodles, meat (if using), soy sauce, sugar, and the remaining ½ tablespoon sesame oil. Stir to combine, and cook for another 2 minutes.

5. Season with salt or more soy sauce, if needed.

6. Serve among 4 plates. If using sesame seeds, add them after plating.

INGREDIENT TIP: Thinly sliced brisket works well in this dish, and Korean barbecued beef (*bulgogi*) is used often. In a pinch, chunks of rotisserie chicken, strips of omelet, or fried tofu pieces are good protein additions.

KIMCHI FRIED RICE

김치볶음밥 *kimchi bokkeumbap*

Kimchi fried rice is usually a home-cooked comfort food, but you'll also see it at casual Korean eateries. At home, it's a great way to use up older or leftover kimchi. Quick, easy, and cheap to make, *kimchi bokkeumbap* is simple Korean home cooking at its best. Everyone has their own version, since there's no right way to make this, and everyone's favorite is usually based on the kimchi fried rice their mom made for them when they were growing up. This is the way I usually make it at home, because the butter gives it a nice, satisfying richness. *Serves 4*

PREP TIME: 30 MINUTES / COOK TIME: 10 MINUTES

Vegetarian-Friendly

⅓ cup thinly sliced beef, SPAM, pork, bacon, or ham

1 cup kimchi, drained and chopped (preferably made with napa cabbage)

½ sweet onion, chopped

1 tablespoon vegetable oil

1 tablespoon butter, divided

1 tablespoon finely chopped garlic

1 tablespoon soy sauce

3 cups cooked rice

Salt

4 fried eggs

SUBSTITUTION TIP: Omit the meat if you are making a vegetarian version.

SUBSTITUTION TIP: If you like a "wetter" version, add 1 or 2 tablespoons of gochujang. You can also reserve a few tablespoons of kimchi juice and add it to the mixture.

1. If using American bacon, sauté briefly in a large, dry skillet and omit the vegetable oil from the next step. If using any other meat, start with step 2.

2. Stir-fry the kimchi and onion in the vegetable oil in a large skillet over medium heat for 2 minutes.

3. When the vegetables begin to look transparent, add ½ tablespoon of the butter along with the garlic and soy sauce and stir-fry for 2 to 3 minutes.

4. Add the meat, and continue to stir-fry until cooked through. Turn the heat off but leave the pan on the burner.

5. Add the rice and the remaining ½ tablespoon butter, and mix well to combine. Taste, and add salt if needed.

6. Serve topped with a fried egg on top of each serving.

PUMPKIN PORRIDGE

호박죽 *hobakjuk*

This fall or winter recipe makes the most of seasonal sweet squashes and pumpkins, and is a soothing breakfast, lunch, dinner, or snack. You can make it with any sweet squash or pumpkin. Unlike other Korean rice porridges (*yuks*), you can make this with glutinous rice powder or glutinous rice, which is a very sticky sweet rice (called *chapsal* in Korean). *Serves 6 to 8*

PREP TIME: 10 MINUTES / COOK TIME: 40 MINUTES

Vegetarian-Friendly,
Vegan-Friendly, Gluten-Free

2½ cups water

1½- to 2-pound Korean pumpkin or Kabocha squash, seeded and peeled, and thinly sliced (about 7 cups)

1 cup glutinous rice powder

¼ cup sugar

Salt

1. Bring the water to a boil in a stockpot over high heat. Reduce the heat to medium, add the pumpkin slices, and cook until tender, about 30 minutes.

2. With a wooden spatula or spoon, mash the pumpkin into the water left in the pot.

3. Reduce the heat to low and stir in the rice powder, sugar, and season with salt, stirring constantly to avoid burning.

4. Raise the heat to high and bring to a boil. Remove from the heat.

5. Serve hot.

INGREDIENT TIP: Don't use the big, round orange pumpkins we carve into jack-o'-lanterns for this dish, because they are watery, pithy, and not very sweet. You can make this dish with canned pumpkin with perfect results, because canned pumpkin in America is usually a mix of pumpkin and different squashes. When selecting canned pumpkin in the baking aisle, be sure not to grab "pumpkin pie filling," because it has added pie spices.

CHICKEN AND RICE PORRIDGE

닭죽 *dakjuk*

Juk (rice porridge) is often fed to the elderly, babies, and anyone who is sick in Korea, but it's also a delicious way to stretch a little rice. It's soothing, comforting, and very good for you. There are endless variations, and you can make it with almost any vegetables, seafood, or meat that you wish. *Serves 3*

PREP TIME: 1 HOUR / COOK TIME: 40 MINUTES

2 cups rice

2 tablespoons toasted sesame oil

5 cups low-sodium chicken broth

1 clove garlic, minced

1 cup shredded poached or roasted chicken, for garnish

2 scallions, finely chopped, for garnish

Toasted sesame seeds, for garnish

Soy sauce, for serving

1. Rinse the rice and soak for 1 hour. Drain.

2. In a stockpot over medium-high heat, stir-fry the rice with the sesame oil for 2 minutes. Add the chicken broth and stir to mix. Raise the heat to high, bring to a boil, and lower the heat to medium and let simmer for 10 minutes.

3. Stir in the garlic and continue to cook for another 20 minutes, or until the rice breaks down and the porridge is thick. Stir a few times during cooking.

4. Serve garnished with shredded chicken, scallions, and sesame seeds, and offer soy sauce alongside.

COOKING TIP: You can make juk even if you have only a small amount of leftover rice. Simmer the leftover rice with the same amount of water, and then keep adding water until it becomes the consistency you like.

Chapter Nine

FISH AND SEAFOOD

Surrounded by the ocean, Korea naturally has a cuisine full of fish, shellfish, and sea vegetables. The most traditional seafood broth is made of very small anchovies, and fish paste is one of the essential seasonings in making kimchi.

I've tried to include a variety of different seafood dishes here, and the good thing about many of these recipes is that you can customize them. You can use flounder, halibut, or sole in the recipes that call for cod or white fish, and you can use clams or mussels instead of cockles if you can't find them.

ABALONE PORRIDGE

 전복죽 *jeonbokjuk*

Abalone porridge traditionally was made and enjoyed in the southern coastal parts of Korea and especially on Cheju Island, but today it's a comfort food for most Koreans. Rice porridge, in general, is what chicken soup is to Americans—a soothing, restorative meal. *Serves 4*

PREP TIME: 3 HOURS / COOK TIME: 1 HOUR

Gluten-Free

1 cup rice

1 tablespoon toasted sesame oil

½ cup abalone, removed from shell, cleaned, and cut into thin trips

6 cups water

Soy sauce, Seasoned Soy Sauce (page 49), or gluten-free soy sauce, for serving

1. Soak the rice for 3 hours before cooking.

2. Heat the sesame oil in a deep saucepan or stockpot over medium heat, add the abalone, and gently stir-fry.

3. Add the rice along with the water. Bring to a boil and then immediately reduce the heat to low, cover the pan, and simmer gently for about 40 minutes, or until the juk becomes the thickness you like. Stir from time to time and watch that it doesn't bubble over.

4. Serve with soy sauce or Seasoned Soy Sauce on the side, for seasoning.

TIP: This used to be a special occasion dish, but now with the popularity of farmed abalone, people eat it more regularly and you can find it on some Korean restaurant menus.

KING PRAWN SALAD
WITH PINE NUT DRESSING

These king prawns are a special side dish, and they are the star in this refreshing, cold Korean salad. You can also make this with regular shrimp if you can't find king prawns. The plating won't be quite as impressive, but it will still taste fantastic. You can grind the pine nuts in a blender or food processor. *Serves 3 as a side dish*

PREP TIME: 15 MINUTES / COOK TIME: 15 MINUTES

For the dressing

¼ cup ground pine nuts

1 tablespoon lemon juice

2 teaspoons toasted sesame oil

½ teaspoon salt

Dash of white pepper

For the prawn salad

1 lemon wedge

6 jumbo shrimp or king prawns, cleaned and deveined, but with shell left on

1 kirby cucumber or pickling cucumber, julienned

1 teaspoon sea salt

2 teaspoons mirin

3½ ounces bamboo shoots, soaked and sliced

¼ Korean pear, julienned

TO MAKE THE DRESSING

In a small bowl, whisk together the pine nuts, lemon juice, sesame oil, salt, and pepper. Set aside.

TO MAKE THE PRAWN SALAD

1. Squeeze the lemon over the prawns and then put them in a steamer basket over boiling water, cover, and steam for 6 to 8 minutes. Let cool.

2. While the prawns are steaming, sprinkle the cucumber with sea salt and let stand for 5 minutes. Then squeeze gently between your hands to remove excess liquid.

3. Shell and halve the prawns lengthwise.

4. In a medium bowl, mix the mirin, cucumber, sea salt, bamboo shoots, and pear with half of the dressing.

5. Mound the vegetable mixture on a serving platter, top with the prawns, and drizzle the remaining dressing over the top.

SEASONED COCKLES

꼬막무침 *kkomangmuchim*

This seasonal Korean dish is popular in the summer. Make this when you have access to great cockles (which are small clams), and feel free to substitute clams or mussels if you can't find cockles. This recipe makes a gorgeous side dish or appetizer for a dinner party. *Serves 4*

PREP TIME: 2 HOURS, 10 MINUTES / COOK TIME: 20 MINUTES

For the sauce

¼ cup soy sauce

1 teaspoon sugar

1 tablespoon gochugaru

2 teaspoons toasted sesame oil

1 tablespoon sesame seeds

2 teaspoons minced garlic

2 scallions, finely chopped

1 red chile, like Korean, finely chopped

1 green chile, like Korean or jalapeño, finely chopped

For the cockles

3 cups cockles, cleaned and scrubbed

8 cups water, divided

2 tablespoons salt

¼ cup sake, plus 1 tablespoon

1 tablespoon mirin

TIP: You can use this sauce for any shellfish, including clams or shrimp.

TO MAKE THE SAUCE

In a small bowl, combine the soy sauce, sugar, gochugaru, sesame oil, and sesame seeds with the garlic, scallions, and chiles. Set aside.

TO MAKE THE COCKLES

1. In a large pot, combine the cockles, 4 cups of water, and salt and let sit in the refrigerator for 1 to 2 hours to expel sand and debris.

2. Rinse the cockles well under cold water.

3. In a stockpot, combine the cockles and the remaining 4 cups water, the sake, and the mirin. Bring to a boil over high heat and cook until the first few cockle shells open up, 5 to 10 minutes. Drain in a colander, trying to separate the cockles so they are not in a heap. Cool for about 10 minutes, or when they're cool enough to handle.

4. Using a metal spoon or knife, remove the top shell of each cockle.

5. Arrange the cockles, still in their bottom shells, on a serving platter and spoon some of the sauce into each.

6. Serve cold.

SPICY RAW BLUE CRABS

양념/간장 게장 *yangnyeom ganjang gejang*

These salty, pickled raw blue crabs are a prized Korean side dish. The traditional way of making this dish is much more salted than the recipe here, because Koreans use this method for preserving raw crabs for a very long time. This less salty but still flavorful dish is adapted for everyday eating, and my favorite part is spooning some of the sauce over my rice after all the crabmeat has been sucked from the shell. *Serves 6 as a side dish*

PREP TIME: 1 HOUR, PLUS 24 HOURS TO MARINATE / COOK TIME: 0

Gluten-Free

1½ pounds blue crab

6 garlic cloves, minced

1-inch piece fresh peeled ginger, grated

2 scallions, halved lengthwise and cut into 1-inch pieces

¼ cup gochugaru

¼ cup sugar

5 Korean green chiles, seeded and sliced into thirds

1 cup Anchovy Stock (page 46)

1 cup soy sauce or gluten-free soy sauce

1. Remove the top shells of the crabs. With a heavy, sharp knife, cut the crabs down the middle. Remove the gills. Remove the orange and yellow insides, keeping just the crabmeat.

2. Cut each section of the crabs into two pieces so they are in quarters.

3. In a large bowl, mix together the garlic, ginger, scallions, gochugaru, sugar, and chiles with the anchovy stock and the soy sauce.

4. Add the crabs to the seasoning mixture, cover, and marinate for 24 hours in the refrigerator.

5. Serve as a cold side dish.

SUBSTITUTION TIP: If you like this very salty and not as spicy-sweet, then use half the amount of gochugaru and sugar.

BRAISED FISH

This lovely recipe always makes the older crowd happy, and it's an easy one to convert. In this recipe, you can use striped bass, cod, halibut, red snapper, or any other firm-fleshed fish. My recipe is light on the spice, but you can easily add gochujang to the sauce for a thicker, spicier flavor. *Serves 4*

PREP TIME: 15 MINUTES / COOK TIME: 25 MINUTES

Gluten-Free

For the sauce

3 garlic cloves, thinly sliced

¼-inch piece ginger, peeled and thinly sliced

1 red Korean chile, cut diagonally into ½-inch pieces

3 cups water

¼ cup soy sauce or gluten-free soy sauce

1 tablespoon sugar

1 tablespoon rice cooking wine

2 teaspoons toasted sesame oil

2 tablespoons gochugaru

For the fish

1 large Korean radish, sliced into 1-inch-long rectangles (about ½-inch thick)

½ onion, sliced

2 pounds firm-fleshed fish (like halibut, cod, red snapper, or sea bass), cut into 2-inch pieces

5 scallions, sliced into 1-inch pieces

TO MAKE THE SAUCE

In a medium bowl, combine the garlic, ginger, chile, water, soy sauce, sugar, rice wine, sesame oil, and gochugaru and mix well.

TO MAKE THE FISH

1. In a stockpot over medium-high heat, mix the radish, onion, and the sauce mixture together and bring to a boil.

2. Add the fish on top of the vegetables, gently stir to mix, and again bring to a boil. Reduce the heat to low and simmer for about 15 minutes, or until the radish is tender. Baste the fish frequently, but try not to disturb it too much while cooking so that it doesn't fall apart.

3. Add the scallions about 1 to 2 minutes before the end of the cooking time.

4. Serve immediately.

VARIATION TIP: For everyday meals, I like the simpler version of this braised fish dish with just radish, fish, and scallions. But don't be shy—flavor it with mushrooms and a variety of chiles or bell peppers if you wish.

PAN-FRIED FISH FILLETS

생선전 *saengseonjeon*

I think of this as a mom dish because I love when my mom makes it, but it's good for any age and as an appetizer at a party. I usually do this with fresh flounder or cod, but almost any white fish works well in this recipe. *Jeon* (or *jun*) refers to any food that is battered and then pan-fried. It could be pieces of meat, fish, or vegetables, like scallion pancakes (*pa jun*). *Serves 4*

PREP TIME: 10 MINUTES / COOK TIME: 15 MINUTES

1 pound fresh flounder or cod, rinsed,
    patted dry, and cut into 2-inch pieces

1 tablespoon sea salt, divided

2 eggs

1 teaspoon freshly ground black pepper

3 tablespoons flour

1 tablespoon vegetable oil

Sensational Soy Dipping Sauce
    (page 48) (optional)

INGREDIENT TIP: The best option is a fresh fish with delicate white flesh like flounder, cod, pollock, sea perch, halibut, or yellow croaker, but even frozen fish tastes good cooked this way.

COOKING TIP: This fish is wonderful served with a spicy dipping sauce or a chili sauce like Sriracha. You may wish to decrease the amount of salt in the recipe to 1 to 2 teaspoons, though, since the sauces are salty.

1. Lightly salt the fish on all sides.

2. In a medium shallow bowl, whisk the eggs with the remaining salt and the pepper.

3. Put the flour in another shallow bowl next to the egg mixture.

4. Heat a bit of the vegetable oil in a medium skillet over medium heat. Dip each fish piece first into the flour to coat, then into the egg mixture, and then gently put it in the skillet. Don't crowd the pan. You might have to do this in batches, adding more oil as necessary.

5. Serve with soy dipping sauce, if desired.

JELLYFISH SALAD

해파리냉채 *haepari naengchae*

Although they can be pests if you're swimming in the ocean, jellyfish make a delicious salad. This dish is easy to make at home and has a nice tang from the mustard dressing. This is one traditional Korean dish that I've never wanted to modernize—it's so fresh, good, and balanced. I don't think we ever ate this jellyfish salad regularly at home, but I grew up eating it at parties, weddings, and other celebratory Korean gatherings. I didn't find out that the crunchy, chewy part was jellyfish until I was in my teens, and it's because the crunchy, chewy jellyfish adds a lot of texture to the dish but doesn't taste particularly "fishy." You can buy jellyfish, salted or unsalted, at Korean and other Asian grocery stores. *Serves 4*

PREP TIME: 30 MINUTES / COOK TIME: 0

4 ounces salted jellyfish, shredded

4 ounces imitation crabmeat, torn into pieces

6 ounces kirby or Japanese cucumber, seeded and julienned

½ carrot, julienned

1 tablespoon lemon juice

3 tablespoons rice vinegar

3 tablespoons sugar

1 tablespoon spicy Korean mustard

1 teaspoon salt

1 tablespoon minced garlic

1 tablespoon toasted sesame seeds

VARIATION TIP: This is a gorgeous salad with a lot of different textures. For variety, you can add thinly sliced red and orange bell peppers and sliced red cabbage for a rainbow of colors.

1. Soak the jellyfish in cold water for about 30 minutes to remove the salt. Remove from the water and spread it out in a colander to drain.

2. Prepare an ice water bath (a large bowl containing cold water and ice cubes). Pour very hot water over the jellyfish in the colander, and then immediately dunk the jellyfish in the ice water bath.

3. Drain the jellyfish again in the colander and pat dry with paper towels.

4. In a large bowl, put the jellyfish, imitation crabmeat, cucumber, and carrot. Season with the lemon juice, rice vinegar, sugar, mustard, salt, garlic, and sesame seeds, and toss to combine.

5. Serve immediately, or after it's been chilled for 2 hours.

SPICY SQUID WITH VEGETABLES

오징어볶음 *ojingeo bokkeum*

This is an awesomely spicy squid dish that is a popular Korean street food, home-cooked dish, and drinking snack. It's perfect with rice to cut the spice, but you can easily cut down the amount of gochugaru (chile flakes) in this if you don't want it too spicy. *Serves 4*

PREP TIME: 15 MINUTES / COOK TIME: 10 MINUTES

Gluten-Free

¼ cup soy sauce or gluten-free soy sauce

3 tablespoons gochugaru

1 tablespoon sugar

1 tablespoon vegetable oil

1 medium sweet onion, sliced

1 large carrot, thinly sliced on the bias

8 scallions, cut into 1-inch pieces

2 Korean chiles, thinly sliced

6 garlic cloves, minced

1½ pounds squid, cleaned and cut into 2-inch strips

2 teaspoons toasted sesame oil

1. In a small bowl, mix together the soy sauce, gochugaru, and sugar.

2. Heat a deep large skillet or wok over high heat. Add the vegetable oil and the onion, and stir-fry for 1 to 2 minutes.

3. Add the carrot, scallions, chiles, and garlic, and stir-fry for 2 minutes.

4. Pour the soy sauce mixture into the vegetables, add the squid and sesame oil, and mix together. Stir-fry for another 3 minutes.

5. Serve hot.

SUBSTITUTION TIP: This is spicy, so you may want to use fewer chiles or hot pepper flakes. You can also increase the sweetness of the sauce with some honey and/or mirin.

BROILED MACKEREL

고등어구이 *godeungeo gui*

Koreans love broiled or grilled fish that is either cooked whole or sliced in half and cooked until the skin is crisp and sizzling. Oily fish like mackerel stand up perfectly to high heat. You can make this recipe easily in a toaster oven on the broiler setting, and it's mess-free and fuss-free. *Serves 2 as a main dish or 4 as a side dish*

PREP TIME: 10 MINUTES / COOK TIME: 15 MINUTES

Gluten-Free

Vegetable oil for the baking sheet

2 teaspoons salt

8 ounces mackerel, whole or deboned with head and tail removed, with skin on

1 lemon wedge

1. Preheat the broiler and lightly oil a baking sheet.

2. Sprinkle the salt over the fish on both sides. Let stand for 10 minutes, and then rinse in cold water. Pat dry with a paper towel, and put on the prepared baking sheet.

3. Put under broiler and cook for 2 to 3 minutes on each side. The skin will get a little crispy.

4. Squeeze the lemon over the fish just before serving.

INGREDIENT TIP: Ask the butcher at the fish counter to remove the backbone, head, and tail, so that you have two fillets of the mackerel with the skin on.

SERVING TIP: If you're making this recipe for guests and want it to look nice, serve this on a platter on a bed of raw onions and thinly sliced lemon rounds with Scallion Salad (page 105) on the side.

PAN-FRIED WHOLE FISH

생선구이 *saengseon gui*

Eating the whole fish is very common in Korea, since nose-to-tail
has never gone out of style. This deceptively simple recipe
cooks up a fish that is crispy on the outside and juicy and tender on
the inside. I often make this dish when I'm hosting multigenerational
dinner parties; my aunts and uncles always appreciate it. *Serves 4*

PREP TIME: 15 MINUTES / COOK TIME: 10 MINUTES

3 tablespoons soju (Korean rice liquor) or sake

2 tablespoons crushed, minced garlic

½ teaspoon salt

¼ teaspoon freshly ground black pepper

2 medium-sized yellow croakers, scaled,
  fins removed, cleaned and rinsed

¼ cup all-purpose flour

1½ tablespoons glutinous rice powder

1 tablespoon cornstarch

Peanut oil for cooking

1. In a large bowl, combine the soju, garlic, salt, and pepper.

2. Coat the fish with the soju mixture and let sit for 15 minutes.

3. In another large shallow bowl, mix together the flour, rice powder, and cornstarch.

4. Dip the fish into the flour mixture, coating both sides evenly.

5. In a deep large skillet or wok, put at least ⅛ inch peanut oil and heat over medium-high heat. Add the fish and cook until both sides are nicely browned, about 3 to 5 minutes per side, adding more oil if necessary.

6. Transfer to a paper towel–lined plate.

7. Serve hot.

INGREDIENT TIP: This is a traditional Korean way to cook yellow croaker (*jogi* or yellow corvina), but I've also substituted grouper and striped bass with good results.

CHILLED SQUID AND SEAWEED SALAD

오징어미역냉채 *ojingeo miyuk naengchae*

This spicy-sweet seafood salad features parboiled squid, seaweed, cucumber, and onions. I like to add jicama to this salad (and other Korean cold dishes) because it has a nice crunch and mild flavor, and it offers a nice counterpoint to the bold dressing. *Serves 4 as a side dish*

PREP TIME: 20 MINUTES / COOK TIME: 1 MINUTE

Gluten-Free

½ cup dried wakame seaweed (*miyuk*)

1 medium squid (about 1 pound), cleaned and cut into 2-inch pieces

2 teaspoons gochugaru

1 tablespoon gochujang or gluten-free gochujang

1 tablespoon soy sauce or gluten-free soy sauce

1 teaspoon toasted sesame oil

1 tablespoon sugar

2 tablespoons rice vinegar

1 kirby cucumber or pickling cucumber, thinly sliced

¼ medium red onion, thinly sliced

½ small jicama, peeled and thinly sliced

1 small green chile, like Korean or jalapeño, seeded and thinly sliced

1 scallion, finely chopped

Salt

Freshly ground black pepper

1. Soak the seaweed in water for 15 minutes. Drain well, and if not already in small pieces, cut into 1-inch pieces.

2. Prepare an ice water bath (a large bowl filled with cold water and ice).

3. Bring a medium pot of water to a boil over medium-high heat. Add the squid and parboil for about 30 seconds, then immediately plunge it into the ice water bath to stop cooking. Drain well, patting dry if needed.

4. In a large bowl, combine the gochugaru, gochujang, soy sauce, sesame oil, sugar, and vinegar and mix well.

5. Add the cucumber, onion, jicama, chile, and scallion to the bowl, along with the squid. Season with salt and pepper. Toss to combine.

6. Serve immediately.

INGREDIENT TIP: If you can't find jicama, you can substitute radish, but reduce the amount, because of radish's peppery flavor.

CLASSIC STEAMED WHITE FISH

생선찜 *saengseon jjim*

This recipe is one of my absolute favorite ways to make and eat white fish fillets, as the fish is delicately seasoned and tender. It is traditionally a Chinese preparation, but goes well with Korean meals, and can also be tweaked to include some preferred Korean ingredients. If you go to a Korean market, you'll see the seafood still alive and swimming. Get the freshest fish you can find when making this dish. *Serves 4*

PREP TIME: 10 MINUTES / COOK TIME: 15 MINUTES

Gluten-Free

4 (4-ounce) white fish fillets,
    like flounder, sea bass, or red snapper

2 tablespoons soy sauce or
    gluten-free soy sauce

1 tablespoon mirin

1 tablespoon very finely sliced
    peeled fresh ginger

1 tablespoon very finely sliced scallion

1 teaspoon toasted sesame oil

1. Pat the fish dry with paper towels.

2. In a small bowl, mix the soy sauce, mirin, ginger, scallion, and sesame oil.

3. Drizzle the sauce mixture over the fish pieces.

4. Put the fish in a steamer over boiling water and steam, covered, for 7 to 8 minutes, or until the fish is opaque and starts to flake.

5. Serve immediately.

COOKING TIP: If you don't have a steamer, you can put the fish in a heat-proof dish in a larger pot filled with ½-inch of boiling water.

SUBSTITUTION TIP: You can vary the flavors and aromatics in this dish. I sometimes change it up with shallots, garlic, and/or lemon.

SOY-HONEY GRILLED SALMON

Broiled salmon is easy to make as long as you make sure that you don't overcook it. For a crowd or a more impressive display, make this with a whole side fillet of salmon instead. Although this is not a traditional Korean dish, it is a quick and always satisfying way to enjoy some fish for dinner. *Serves 2 as a main dish or 4 as a side dish*

PREP TIME: 15 MINUTES / COOK TIME: 10 MINUTES

Gluten-Free

Vegetable oil for the pan

½ cup soy sauce or gluten-free soy sauce

¼ cup sugar

¼ cup honey

1 teaspoon vegetable or olive oil

1 pound salmon (cut into 4-ounce fillets or steaks), with skin on

1. Preheat the broiler and coat a 9-inch square baking pan lightly with cooking oil.

2. In a small bowl, mix together the soy sauce, sugar, honey, and vegetable oil. Brush the soy-honey glaze over the salmon (reserve any extra glaze), coating it on both sides, and let stand for 15 minutes.

3. Put the salmon, skin-side down, on the prepared pan and drizzle any remaining glaze over the top.

4. Broil the fish on the top rack for 6 to 8 minutes. Turn once halfway through cooking if you're using salmon steaks.

5. Serve immediately.

COOKING TIP: This is a versatile recipe, which is also wonderful on the grill. For grilled salmon, prepare as directed and grill for about 5 minutes per side.

RICE WITH FISH EGGS

알밥 *al bap*

Al bap is a delicious type of mixed rice dish (bibimbap) made unique by the inclusion of fish eggs. In restaurants, it is often made and served in the traditional Korean stoneware bowls so that the rice becomes hot, crisp, and roasted. But this mixed rice with caviar dish is also delicious made in regular bowls. Like other types of bibimbap, you can make this dish with the vegetables you wish. *Serves 4*

PREP TIME: 30 MINUTES / COOK TIME: 10 MINUTES

Gluten-Free

2 cups Napa Cabbage Kimchi (page 54), squeezed of excess liquid and chopped

1½ tablespoons toasted sesame oil, plus ½ tablespoon

2 teaspoons sugar

2 teaspoons soy sauce or gluten-free soy sauce

4 cups cooked Korean rice

½ pound salted pollock eggs

6 slices perilla leaves (kkaennip, shiso, or sesame leaves), thinly sliced

4 eggs, fried sunny-side up

1. In a medium bowl, mix the chopped kimchi with ½ tablespoon of the sesame oil, sugar, and soy sauce.

2. In a large bowl, season the rice with the remaining 1½ tablespoons sesame oil.

3. Put the rice into 4 bowls, and arrange the fish eggs, sliced perilla leaves, and the kimchi mixture on top. Top each bowl with a fried egg.

4. Serve. Each diner should mix the ingredients in the bowl before eating.

SPICY MONKFISH STEW

아구찜 *agujjim*

Monkfish is meaty and full of sweet flavor, and it makes a delicious hearty stew. Some restaurants seem to make this with more gochujang than doenjang, but I like it with more bean-paste flavor. Feel free to swap the proportions of these two ingredients if you like it the other way. *Serves 4*

PREP TIME: 15 MINUTES / COOK TIME: 35 MINUTES

Gluten-Free

2 tablespoons doenjang or
    gluten-free doenjang

1 tablespoon gochujang or
    gluten-free gochujang

1 tablespoon gochugaru

Salt

6 cups Anchovy Stock (page 46),
    or store-bought seafood broth

1 small zucchini, cut into 2-inch slices

1 small sweet onion, sliced

1 small daikon, cut into 2-inch pieces

5 ounces fresh shiitake
    mushrooms, thinly sliced

1 to 1½ pounds monkfish, cut
    into 2-inch chunks

1 (14-ounce) package of mung bean
    or sweet potato noodles, cooked
    according to the package directions

1 scallion, chopped, for garnish

1. In a stockpot, mix together the doenjang, gochujang, gochugaru, a pinch of salt, and the anchovy stock and set the pot over medium-high heat. Once the seasonings are dissolved in the stock, add the zucchini, onion, daikon, and mushrooms and bring up to a boil. Reduce the heat to low and simmer for 10 minutes.

2. Add the monkfish and simmer gently for about 15 minutes, or until the fish is cooked through.

3. To serve, divide the noodles among 4 large soup bowls and ladle the stew over the noodles. Garnish each serving with scallions.

INGREDIENT TIP: These noodles might be labeled as cellophane noodles, glass noodles, or Chinese vermicelli at the Asian grocery store.

STEAMED SKATE FISH

홍어찜 *hongeojjim*

Skate wings are tender and have a delightful taste. This easy recipe is a foolproof way to make a delicious meal out of skate. At Asian markets, you can find "pan-ready" skate wings already skinned and filleted for you. *Serves 4*

PREP TIME: 10 MINUTES / COOK TIME: 25 MINUTES

Gluten-Free

Salt

Freshly ground black pepper

2 large skate wings, skinned, filleted, and rinsed

2 tablespoons good-quality sake (or rice cooking wine)

2 tablespoons toasted sesame oil

3 eggs, lightly beaten

1 scallion, thinly sliced on the bias, for garnish

Korean chile thread or gochugaru, for garnish

1. Sprinkle salt and pepper on both sides of the skate wings.

2. Put the skate wings in a steamer set over boiling water, cover, and steam for about 10 minutes.

3. Pour the sake and sesame oil over fish and cover again. Steam for an additional 5 to 10 minutes (depending on thickness), until the fish is cooked through (is opaque and flakes when poked with the tip of a sharp knife).

4. Meanwhile, cook the eggs in a nonstick skillet into a thin, flat omelet, and then slice it into thin strips.

5. Serve the fish hot, garnished with the egg strips, scallion, and chili thread.

INGREDIENT TIP: Skate are closely related to sharks. They have large pectoral fins that we refer to as wings.

INGREDIENT TIP: Korean dried chile threads, which are thin strings of red pepper about 2 inches long, are an attractive garnish that also add a little bit of spice to dishes.

Chapter Ten

POULTRY AND MEAT

Although Koreans have eaten beef, pork, and poultry since ancient times, it wasn't until the last fifty years that meat was eaten regularly in large quantities. Meat was reserved for special occasions, or was used in small quantities to give flavor to dishes. Although modern Korean meals include meat regularly, you don't need to make much meat per person because other side dishes are served with every meal.

The most common Korean cooking techniques for meat and poultry are braising, grilling, and stir-frying, and a lot of flavor comes from sweet and smoky marinades and seasonings.

ROASTED CHICKEN WINGS

통닭 *tongdak*

Chicken wings are easy to eat and snack on, and they're good for parties, drinking snacks, and appetizers. These little savory bites are juicy, spicy, and sweet, and it's hard to just eat one. *Tongdak* is often deep-fried in Korea, but these oven-cooked wings are easier to make and more healthful. *Serves 4*

PREP TIME: 15 MINUTES, PLUS 1 HOUR TO MARINATE / COOK TIME: 1 HOUR

1 inch fresh ginger, peeled and minced

2 teaspoons toasted sesame oil

¼ cup plus 2 tablespoons soy sauce

3 tablespoons sugar

3 tablespoons honey

5 garlic cloves, minced

½ small sweet onion, minced

1 tablespoon gochujang

2 pounds chicken wings and drumettes

VARIATION TIP: Serve these with celery sticks, carrot sticks, and blue cheese dressing for a Korean twist on Buffalo wings.

1. In a large bowl, mix the ginger, sesame oil, soy sauce, sugar, honey, garlic, onion, and gochujang together. Stir until well combined.

2. Add the chicken and toss to coat well. Marinate the chicken in the refrigerator for at least 1 hour (2 to 3 hours would be better).

3. Preheat the oven to 400°F.

4. Heat a large nonstick skillet over medium-high heat.

5. Remove the chicken from the marinade (reserving the marinade) and brown the chicken on all sides.

6. Transfer the chicken to a shallow roasting pan, and pour the reserved marinade over the top.

7. Bake in the oven for 40 to 50 minutes, turning once and basting with the sauce after 20 minutes.

8. Serve immediately.

BRAISED CHICKEN AND POTATOES

닭도리탕 *dakdoritang*

This Korean chicken stew is Korean home cooking at its best, and it's simple and easy to make with great results. Simmering makes the chicken tender, and the sauce has a spicy kick. It hits the spot every time. Serve it over white rice with an extra scoop of sauce for an easy and comforting meal. *Serves 4*

PREP TIME: 10 MINUTES / COOK TIME: 40 MINUTES

2 pounds boneless, skinless chicken thighs cut into large pieces

1 large carrot, cut into 2-inch pieces

2 yellow onions, cut into large chunks

2 large potatoes, cut into large chunks

4 garlic cloves, finely chopped

⅔ cup soy sauce

⅓ cup water

3 tablespoons gochujang

1 tablespoon gochugaru

1 chopped scallion, for garnish (optional)

1. In a large stockpot over medium-high heat, combine the chicken, carrot, onions, and potatoes.

2. In a small bowl, mix together the garlic, soy sauce, water, gochujang, and gochugaru. Whisk to combine.

3. Pour the sauce mixture over the chicken and vegetables and bring to a boil. Reduce the heat to low and simmer for 40 minutes, or until the sauce has thickened.

4. Add the scallions, if using. Serve hot.

VARIATION TIP: Although this is a simple, comforting stew, you can make it special in a few different ways. Swap the potatoes for sweet potatoes or add green and red bell peppers and green and red chiles for a more colorful dish.

MARINATED GRILLED CHICKEN

This basic Korean grilled chicken in a sweet soy marinade is good for any-time, and is a lip-smacking dinner or backyard barbecue recipe. Once you master this recipe, it is sure to become a regular in your rotation. You can also use the marinade for chicken drumsticks and chicken breasts. *Serves 4*

PREP TIME: 15 MINUTES, PLUS 2 HOURS TO MARINATE / COOK TIME: 20 MINUTES

¼ cup toasted sesame oil

3 tablespoons soy sauce

2 tablespoons light brown sugar

2 medium shallots, finely chopped

1 tablespoon finely grated peeled fresh ginger

4 garlic cloves, minced

4 teaspoons mirin

2 teaspoons gochugaru

Salt

Freshly ground black pepper

2 pounds boneless, skinless chicken thighs, cut into 1-inch pieces

1 head red leaf lettuce, washed and dried with leaves separated, for serving

2 scallions, thinly sliced, for serving

1 teaspoon toasted sesame seeds, for serving

4 cups cooked white rice, preferably short-grain, for serving

Lettuce Wrap Sauce (page 51)

1. In a large bowl, combine the sesame oil, soy sauce, brown sugar, shallots, ginger, garlic, mirin, and gochugaru with a pinch of salt and a pinch of pepper to make the marinade.

2. Add the chicken and toss to coat. Cover and refrigerate for at least 2 hours.

3. Preheat a grill, or cook on a grill pan. Grill the chicken covered in foil for 6 to 8 minutes, turning once during cooking.

4. Serve the grilled chicken with lettuce for wrapping, scallions, sesame seeds, rice, and and Lettuce Wrap Sauce. To eat, put a small dollop of rice, sauce, and a piece of chicken inside a lettuce leaf.

VARIATION TIP: Instead of serving the chicken with lettuce wraps, you can make Korean chicken tacos with this recipe. Serve with warm corn tortillas, shredded cabbage, musaengchae, and scallion kimchi.

STEWED CHICKEN WITH MUSHROOMS

This aromatic braised chicken dish starts on the stove and finishes in the oven. The mushrooms give it a deep, rich flavor. This is an easy, satisfying, and delicious dinner recipe to have in your repertoire, and you can probably get all these ingredients at your local grocery store. *Serves 4*

PREP TIME: 10 MINUTES / COOK TIME: 50 MINUTES

2 tablespoons vegetable or olive oil

1 medium sweet onion, sliced

2 garlic cloves, minced

½ pound shiitake mushrooms, stems removed and cut into thin slices

6 bone-in chicken thighs, skinned

⅓ cup low-sodium chicken broth

3 tablespoons soy sauce

3 tablespoons mirin

2 teaspoons chopped fresh peeled ginger (or ¼ teaspoon ground ginger)

Pinch of salt

Pinch of freshly ground black pepper

1. Preheat the oven to 350°F.

2. Heat 1 tablespoon of oil over medium heat in an ovenproof skillet. Add the onions and cook, stirring frequently, until softened, about 5 minutes.

3. Add the garlic and cook for another 2 minutes.

4. Add the mushrooms and cook until softened, another 2 to 3 minutes.

5. Move the vegetables to the side of the skillet and brown the chicken, about 2 to 3 minutes per side.

6. In a small bowl, whisk together the chicken broth, soy sauce, mirin, ginger, salt, and pepper until well combined.

7. Pour the seasoning mixture over the chicken in the skillet, stirring the ingredients to combine thoroughly.

8. Bake, covered, stirring a few times, until the chicken is tender and the juices run clear when pierced with a sharp knife, about 30 minutes.

SLOW COOKER SHREDDED SESAME CHICKEN

This sesame chicken cooks in the slow cooker and is excellent served over rice or inside lettuce wraps. It is a perfect dish for cookouts and casual get-togethers, since the hands-on time is minimal and it can stay warm until you're ready to serve. *Serves 4*

PREP TIME: 10 MINUTES / COOK TIME: 5 HOURS

¼ cup mirin

2 tablespoons toasted sesame oil

6 garlic cloves

1 teaspoon ground ginger

¼ cup soy sauce

1 tablespoon light brown sugar

2 pounds boneless, skinless chicken breasts, trimmed of fat

2 cups cooked rice, for serving

8 large lettuce leaves, for serving

1. In a large bowl, whisk together the mirin, sesame oil, garlic cloves, ginger, soy sauce, and brown sugar. Add the chicken to the bowl and toss to coat.

2. Transfer the chicken and sauce to the slow cooker, cover with the lid, and cook for 5 hours on low.

3. Transfer the chicken to a cutting board and shred with a fork. Return the shredded chicken to the sauce in the slow cooker and keep warm until ready to serve.

4. Serve hot over rice or inside lettuce wraps.

VARIATION TIP: To use this as the filling for Asian sloppy joe sandwiches, serve on sesame seed buns with shredded lettuce or cabbage. Top with grated cheese, if desired.

BOILED PORK

보쌈 *bo ssam*

This boiled pork dish is a fun way to enjoy good kimchi and pork belly. The name translates to "wrapped," and the bite-size wraps make an excellent appetizer, meal, or drinking snack. Because it's such a communal dish, this is a great thing to serve for a casual get together with friends or for other occasions when you don't want to serve a full Korean meal. *Serves 6 to 8*

PREP TIME: 10 MINUTES / COOK TIME: 80 MINUTES

8 cups water

1 pound pork belly

1 ounce fresh ginger, cut into slices

12 or more whole leaves napa cabbage

Seasoned Radish Strips
   (with *saengchae* sauce, page 91)

Korean fermented, salted shrimp (*saeujeot*)

Lettuce Wrap Sauce (page 51)

STORING TIP: Save some of the liquid you used to boil the pork if there's any chance you'll have leftovers. You can reheat the pork in the liquid the next time you want to eat it.

1. To make the pork, bring a large stockpot of water to a boil over high heat.

2. Add the pork belly and ginger, reduce the heat, cover, and simmer for 1 hour. Remove from the heat and let the pork belly cool in the liquid for about 10 minutes.

3. Remove the pork belly to a carving board and slice it in thirds lengthwise, and then cut each piece into slices that are ¼ inch thick.

4. Discard the cooking liquid and rinse out the pot. Fill the pot about halfway with water and bring to a boil.

5. Add the cabbage leaves and parboil for about 1 minute and then dunk into very cold water. Drain and then slice the cabbage leaves into small pieces.

6. Serve the pork belly slices with the cabbage leaves, seasoned radish, tiny fermented shrimp, and lettuce wrap sauce.

PORK BELLY WITH SESAME DIP

삼겹살 *samgyeopsal*

A popular meat dish for family dinners or at Korean barbecue restaurants,
this is one of the few Korean meat dishes that is not marinated or seasoned.
Pork belly has fatty stripes and is the cut American bacon comes from.
The Korean version is uncured, however, so it is very white and beige in
color. Enjoy this dish with rice, kimchi, and other side dishes. *Serves 3*

PREP TIME: 10 MINUTES / COOK TIME: 10 MINUTES

Gluten-Free

2 tablespoons toasted sesame oil

1 teaspoon fine salt

Freshly ground black pepper

3 to 4 garlic cloves, thinly sliced

2 Korean green chiles, sliced and seeded

1 pound pork belly, thinly sliced

1 head of red or green lettuce, for serving

10 perilla leaves, for serving

1. To make the sesame dip, in a small bowl, mix together the sesame oil and salt, and season with black pepper. Set aside.

2. Heat a grill to medium-high heat.

3. Put the garlic and chiles on the outer edge of the grill and cook until tender, about 4 minutes.

4. Grill the pork belly, flipping once, until the fat is rendered and the pork is browned, about 3 minutes per side.

5. Serve with the sesame dip, lettuce leaves, and perilla leaves for optional wrapping.

COOKING TIP: You can also cook the pork belly in a grill pan on the stove top. We make this on a George Foreman grill at the table with great success.

SPICY SLICED PORK

제육볶음 *jeyuk bokkeum*

This saucy, spicy pork dish can be either grilled or pan-fried. It's great over rice, and is very popular cooked with vegetables like onions, zucchini, and bell peppers. You can also serve this with lettuce leaves to be wrapped with rice into *ssambap*. *Serves 4*

PREP TIME: 30 MINUTES, PLUS 30 MINUTES TO MARINATE / COOK TIME: 10 MINUTES

Gluten-Free

½ sweet onion, finely minced

1 tablespoon minced garlic

1½ teaspoons toasted sesame oil

1 tablespoon soy sauce or gluten-free soy sauce

2 tablespoons gochujang or gluten-free gochujang

2 tablespoons sugar

1 tablespoon mirin

1 teaspoon fresh minced peeled ginger

2 pounds pork butt

INGREDIENT TIP: Pork butt is the best cut for this dish, but you can use a leaner cut if desired.

VARIATION TIP: I didn't grow up eating this very often, but did start enjoying it as an adult. My favorite way to make this now is with boiled rice cake ovals, which add both a chewy texture to the dish and balance the heat nicely.

1. Preheat a grill to medium-high heat, or preheat the broiler.

2. In a medium bowl, mix together the onion, garlic, sesame oil, soy sauce, gochujang, sugar, mirin, and ginger until well-blended.

3. Freeze the pork for 20 minutes, so it hardens and is easier to slice. Slice the pork into very thin pieces, about the thickness of bacon.

4. Add the pork to the bowl with the marinade and let sit for at least 30 minutes.

5. Grill or broil, flipping once, for 4 to 8 minutes, until cooked through. You can also stir-fry the pork in an unoiled skillet for 8 to 10 minutes.

6. Serve hot.

SOYBEAN PASTE PORK

I love the Japanese way of marinating fish and meat with miso, so this is a preparation I love even though it's not as popular as other Korean pork dishes. The bean paste adds great flavor to mild pork cuts such as tenderloin. *Serves 3*

PREP TIME: 10 MINUTES, PLUS 30 MINUTES TO MARINATE / COOK TIME: 10 MINUTES

Gluten-Free

1 pound pork tenderloin

1 tablespoon mirin

1 tablespoon soy sauce or gluten-free soy sauce

1 tablespoon doenjang or gluten-free doenjang

1 tablespoon minced garlic

2 tablespoons sake

1 tablespoon sugar

1 tablespoon toasted sesame oil

1 teaspoon ground sesame seeds

Pinch of freshly ground black pepper

1. If there is a silvery membrane running down the side of the pork tenderloin, trim it. Slice the pork thinly.

2. In a medium bowl, mix together the mirin, soy sauce, doenjang, garlic, sake, sugar, sesame oil, sesame seeds, and pepper until well-combined.

3. Add the pork to the bowl and toss with the marinade. Marinate for 30 minutes.

4. Stir-fry or grill the pork over medium-high heat until cooked through, 6 to 8 minutes.

5. Serve hot.

VARIATION TIP: For a show-stopping grill recipe, use bone-in pork chops marinated in this sauce, and cook on the grill.

SWEET AND SPICY BABY BACK RIBS

돼지갈비 *dwaeji galbi*

These ribs are falling-off-the-bone tender, and although they require some patience since you have to marinate and cook them for a long time, they require very little hands-on time. Because you can make a lot of these at once, this is a good party recipe and is always a hit. *Serves 6 to 8*

PREP TIME: 10 MINUTES, PLUS 5 HOURS TO MARINATE / COOK TIME: 90 MINUTES

½ cup gochujang

2 tablespoons light brown sugar

2 tablespoons lower-sodium soy sauce

2 tablespoons rice wine vinegar

2 teaspoons toasted sesame oil

½ teaspoon salt

1 teaspoon freshly ground black pepper

3 pounds baby back pork ribs,
   cut into individual ribs

SUBSTITUTION TIP: Baby back ribs are popular because they're succulent and so easy to eat, but if you try this with spare ribs or country ribs, you'll get a meatier, and still outstanding result.

1. In a small bowl, whisk together the gochujang, sugar, soy sauce, vinegar, sesame oil, salt, and pepper until well combined.

2. In a large bowl, toss the ribs with half of the marinade. Marinate, in the refrigerator, for at least 5 hours.

3. Preheat the oven to 350°F.

4. Transfer the ribs to a baking dish, discarding the marinade they were in.

5. Bake the ribs on the middle rack, covered with foil, until meat is tender, about 1 hour. Raise the oven temperature to 450°F and roast the ribs, basting occasionally with the reserved half of the marinade, for about 20 to 30 minutes, or until the ribs are nicely browned.

6. Serve immediately.

BEEF SKEWERS WITH RICE CAKES AND SCALLIONS

산적 *sanjeok*

These colorful skewers are festive for special occasions and parties, and they are a convenient finger food for passing or snacking. Although this dish is easy and delicious to make in a skillet, you can also grill these skewers for a smokier flavor. *Serves 4*

PREP TIME: 15 MINUTES, PLUS 30 MINUTES TO MARINATE / COOK TIME: 10 MINUTES

3 tablespoons soy sauce

¼ sweet onion, grated

2 garlic cloves, chopped

1 tablespoon toasted sesame oil

2 teaspoons sugar

Freshly ground black pepper

⅓ pound sirloin steak, cut into strips 3 inches long and ½ inch wide

3 medium-size Korean rice cake cylinders, cut into 2-inch lengths

1 medium carrot, cut into sticks 2 inches long and ⅓ inch wide

10 scallions, cut into 2-inch lengths

2 tablespoons vegetable oil for frying

1. In a medium bowl, mix together the soy sauce, onion, garlic, sesame oil, sugar, and pepper.

2. Add the sliced beef to the sauce and toss to coat. Marinate for at least 30 minutes in the refrigerator.

3. Using a toothpick, skewer the ingredients in this order: beef, rice cake, carrot, and scallion. You should have room to repeat the order twice on each toothpick.

4. Heat the vegetable oil in a medium skillet over medium-high heat. Add the skewered meat and vegetables and cook for 4 to 5 minutes per side, using the remaining sauce if needed.

5. Serve hot.

INGREDIENT TIP: You can make simpler versions of this dish with just steak and scallions, with all vegetables, or with steak and rice cakes.

GRILLED BEEF SHORT RIBS

갈비 | *galbi*

These Korean short ribs are tender, sweet, and full of the flavors of soy and garlic. Called *kalbi* or *galbi*, they are usually served with Lettuce Wrap Sauce (ssamjang, page 51). A spoonful of rice, a piece of galbi, and a dollop of ssamjang wrapped up in lettuce is a divine mouthful of some of the best flavors in Korean cooking. For Koreans, galbi is popular as both picnic food and restaurant food. *Serves 4*

PREP TIME: 15 MINUTES, PLUS 4 HOURS TO MARINATE / COOK TIME: 10 MINUTES

4 garlic cloves, chopped

½ cup soy sauce

¼ cup sugar

1 whole Asian pear, peeled, cored, and puréed or crushed

2 tablespoons honey

2 tablespoons mirin

2 tablespoons toasted sesame oil

2 teaspoons freshly ground black pepper

3 to 4 pounds beef short ribs, flanken cut (see Tip following)

1. In a large bowl, mix together the garlic, soy sauce, sugar, pear, honey, mirin, sesame oil, and black pepper, stirring until the sugar and honey are dissolved. Add the short ribs and stir to coat well. Cover and refrigerate for at least 4 hours or overnight.

2. Preheat the grill to medium heat.

3. Grill the short ribs until well browned, about 3 to 4 minutes per side.

4. To serve, cut between the bones with kitchen shears to make pieces that are easy to eat.

INGREDIENT TIP: Flanken-cut short ribs are also called "LA-Style galbi." The meat is thinly sliced across the bone, so that the meat doesn't have to marinate as long and is tender.

TIP: Some people use Coca-Cola or 7-Up in their meat marinade to help tenderize the meat, and although I don't do that, it is a useful trick if you don't have at least 4 hours to marinate the meat.

SLICED BARBECUED BEEF

불고기| *bulgogi*

Bulgogi is one of the most popular and well-known Korean meat dishes, and is usually the star at backyard barbecues. This thinly sliced steak has a smoky, sweet flavor when broiled or cooked on the grill. It's even delicious stir-fried, and the tender beef can be eaten in anything from Korean "sushi" rolls (*kimbap*) to stir-fried noodles (see Sweet Potato Noodles, page 142). If eating this dish in the traditional way, serve with cooked rice, lettuce leaves, Lettuce Wrap Sauce (page 51), and side dishes. *Serves 4*

PREP TIME: 3 HOURS 30 MINUTES, PLUS 3 HOURS TO MARINATE / COOK TIME: 10 MINUTES

3 tablespoons chopped garlic

3 tablespoons soy sauce

2 tablespoons sugar

1 tablespoon honey

3 tablespoons freshly squeezed Asian pear juice

1 tablespoon mirin

1 tablespoon toasted sesame oil

3 scallions, finely chopped

1 teaspoon freshly ground black pepper

1 pound sirloin steak, thinly sliced

1. In a large bowl, mix together the garlic, soy sauce, sugar, honey, pear juice, mirin, sesame oil, scallions, and pepper and stir until the sugar and honey are dissolved.

2. Add the meat and toss to coat thoroughly with the sauce. Cover and refrigerate for at least 3 hours or overnight. For tougher cuts of meat, marinate the meat longer.

3. Grill (or broil or stir-fry) the beef until well done and caramelized on the outside, about 3 minutes per side.

4. Serve hot.

INGREDIENT TIP: Top sirloin or tenderloin work best, but almost any steak cut will do. The best quality meat will be more tender and will taste the best.

INGREDIENT TIP: If you can, ask the butcher at the meat counter to slice the meat for you in very thin strips. Korean and/or Asian grocery stores will often have pre-sliced bulgogi meat for sale.

INGREDIENT TIP: Asian pears are watery, so you can slice your pears into strips and even squeeze them between your hands to extract the juice. Or you can cut one up and squeeze it in a citrus press.

SUBSTITUTION TIP: This is the most basic recipe. Add some carrots, onions, scallions, and bell peppers, if you wish, for some additional color and flavor.

BRAISED BEEF SHORT RIBS

갈비찜 *galbi jjim*

These decadent Korean braised short ribs are slow-simmered over low heat to a tender and sweet finish. Make this with bone-in ribs, because like Italian osso bucco or Irish stew, *galbi jjim* relies on the stewed bone marrow for its rich flavor. This is a favorite party or celebratory dinner dish, as it's very hearty and rich and adds a lot of depth to a traditional Korean spread. *Serves 4*

PREP TIME: 20 MINUTES / COOK TIME: 1 HOUR

¼ cup plus 1 tablespoon sugar

¼ cup plus 2 tablespoons soy sauce

2 tablespoons mirin

4 garlic cloves, finely chopped

½ onion, grated

3 scallions, finely chopped

1 tablespoon sesame seeds, crushed or whole

1 tablespoon toasted sesame oil

½ Asian pear, peeled, cored, and finely chopped

3 pounds English-cut short ribs (sometimes called thick-cut), rinsed in cold water

2 small potatoes, cut into large chunks

2 medium carrots, cut into 2-inch lengths, or ½ cup baby carrots

1. Score the ribs a few times so they absorb more of the braising liquid.

2. In a large bowl, mix together the sugar, soy sauce, mirin, garlic, onion, scallions, sesame seeds, and sesame oil. Whisk until the sugar is dissolved.

3. In a large heavy-bottomed stockpot over high heat, combine the pear, the ribs, and the braising liquid mixture. Mix well, making sure all the ribs are covered. The liquid will come up to almost half of the level of the ribs in the pot.

4. Cover the pot with a tight-fitting lid and bring just to a boil over high heat. Reduce the heat to low and simmer for at least 1 hour, adding the potatoes and carrots 30 minutes before end of the cooking time and stirring them in gently.

5. Serve hot.

SUBSTITUTION TIP: If you are adding brisket or stew meat for more quantity, then it's best to braise for at least 90 minutes. The goal is for meltingly tender meat that is falling off the bone.

MEAT PATTIES

동그랑땡 *dong gu rang tteng*

In restaurants and stores, these meat patties have many names in both Korean and English. You can call them meat fritters, *kogi jun*, beef patties, and *dhon jeon*. They are simple to make and master, but the well-seasoned meat, tofu, and vegetable patties are bursting with flavor. Because they're bite-size and easy to eat, they're perfect for party finger foods or for lunchboxes. These small meat patties belong to the Korean group of food called *jun-ya*, or vegetables, meat, or seafood that are covered in flour and egg and then pan-fried. *Serves 4 as part of a larger Korean meal*

PREP TIME: 10 MINUTES / COOK TIME: 20 MINUTES

1 pound ground beef

¾ cup medium or firm tofu,
    pressed and squeezed of excess liquid

½ cup finely chopped sweet onion

2 teaspoons minced garlic

1 tablespoon sugar

1 tablespoon toasted sesame oil

2 teaspoons salt

1 tablespoon soy sauce

1 teaspoon freshly ground black pepper

1 tablespoon sesame salt

3 tablespoons all-purpose flour

2 eggs, beaten

VARIATION TIP: These look like mini hamburgers, so you can serve them on Hawaiian sweet rolls as sliders. Top with a little Sriracha Mayo (page 188) and some Asian coleslaw, and you have a perfect little East-West fusion burger.

1. In a large bowl, mix the beef with the tofu, onion, garlic, sugar, sesame oil, salt, soy sauce, pepper, and sesame salt. Mix well to combine.

2. Shape the meat mixture into small flat patties about the size of silver dollar.

3. Heat a large skillet over medium heat.

4. Put the flour in a medium shallow bowl and pour the eggs into a separate medium shallow bowl next to it.

5. Coat the patties first in the flour and then dip into the egg.

6. Carefully put the patties in the hot pan, spooning a small amount of egg mixture onto each patty.

7. After placing all the patties in the pan, turn the heat to medium-low. Cook, turning once, for 3 to 4 minutes per side.

8. Serve hot or warm.

KOREAN-STYLE BEEF TARTARE

육회 *yukhoe*

This Korean beef tartare is gorgeous as an appetizer or as one of the
star dishes in a special occasion dinner. The raw beef, thinly sliced and
seasoned with fragrant spices and seasonings, is served with fresh,
crunchy Asian pears and cucumbers. Since this is a dish of raw meat,
buy the freshest meat possible. Talk to the butcher at your grocery store
or visit a traditional butcher shop to get the freshest beef. *Serves 5*

PREP TIME: 30 MINUTES / COOK TIME: 0

¾ pound fresh high-quality beef like
   tenderloin or filet mignon

2 tablespoons pine nuts

1 Asian pear, cut into matchsticks

1 teaspoon freshly squeezed lemon juice

2 garlic cloves, minced

¼ cup soy sauce

2 tablespoons sugar

1 scallion, chopped

1 tablespoon toasted sesame oil

1 kirby or Persian cucumber,
   cut into matchsticks

1 egg yolk

1 tablespoon sesame seeds

INGREDIENT TIP: Pasteurized eggs are
safe to eat when raw. I also eat organic
or pastured eggs raw. If you are worried
about food safety in organic or pastured
eggs, wash the eggs briefly in soapy water
before cracking them.

1. Freeze the beef for about 20 minutes so
you'll be able to slice it into thin strips.

2. Meanwhile, toast the pine nuts in a
dry skillet over medium-high heat until
beginning to lightly brown and smell aromatic, 3 to 4 minutes.

3. In a small bowl, toss the pear with the
lemon juice so it doesn't brown.

4. In a medium bowl, mix the garlic, pine
nuts, soy sauce, sugar, scallion, and sesame oil together to make the seasoning
mixture.

5. Remove the beef from the freezer and
slice it into very thin strips.

6. In a medium bowl, mix the beef and
seasoning mixture together.

7. On a serving platter, mound the seasoned beef neatly. Arrange the pear and
cucumber slices neatly next to the meat.

8. Make a depression in the top of the
beef and gently slide the egg yolk into it.

9. Serve, sprinkled with sesame seeds.
At the table, break the egg yolk and mix it
with the beef.

Chapter Eleven

FUSION FARE

Trends are a huge part of modern Korean life, and food and fashion fads change constantly and quickly. In this chapter, however, I've included the fusion recipes that have stood the test of time and are now part of the contemporary Korean food scene. Some, like the potato salad (from the Japanese during their colonization of Korea) and the army base stew (invented during the Korean War), are a taste of Korean history. Others, like sweet potato pizza and spicy fried chicken, are Koreanizations of Western foods. The other "KFC," or Korean Fried Chicken, is a popular drinking snack that's here to stay, and the fast and satisfying street foods and snacks listed here are only growing more popular.

KOREAN POTATO SALAD

감자샐러드 *gamjasaelleodeu*

Korean potato salad is a popular side dish in Korea, which surprises
many visitors. Unlike Western versions, it includes fruit, vegetables,
and sometimes ham, and it doesn't have a vinegary component. This
is best made with Kewpie mayonnaise, which is creamier and a
little sweeter than American mayo. *Serves 6 as a side dish*

PREP TIME: 15 MINUTES / COOK TIME: 10 MINUTES

Vegetarian-Friendly

4 to 5 medium potatoes, peeled and cubed

1 small carrot, cut into medium dice

½ small cucumber, cut into medium dice

½ small onion, cut into small dice

Salt

2 hard-boiled eggs, yolks removed
   and cut into small chunks

1 Fuji apple, cut into small chunks

¼ cup diced ham or Canadian bacon (optional)

¾ cup Kewpie mayonnaise

Freshly ground black pepper

VARIATION TIP: This is not just a good side
dish; it's also an incredible sandwich filling. Try it between slices of good bread for
a tasty lunch. I usually omit the ham (or
Canadian bacon) if I'm using it as a side
dish (*banchan*) but I include it if I'm using
it as a sandwich filling.

1. In a large stockpot, cover the potatoes
generously with water and bring to a boil.
After 2 minutes, add the carrot and cook
for another 8 minutes.

2. Meanwhile, put the cucumber and
onion in a colander over a bowl and
sprinkle with salt. Let them sweat for
about 10 minutes.

3. Drain the potatoes and carrot, and let
cool. Put in a large bowl.

4. Gently smash the potatoes with the
back of a fork. Leave some of the potatoes
mostly intact.

5. Rinse the cucumber and onion lightly
and squeeze out excess water with
paper towels.

6. To the potatoes and carrot, add the
cucumber, onion, eggs, apple, ham, and
mayonnaise, and mix gently. Season with
salt and pepper.

INGREDIENT TIP: If you can't find Kewpie
mayonnaise, then Miracle Whip is a good
substitute. You can also use American
mayonnaise if that's what you have
on hand.

KOREAN-STYLE SWEET POTATO PIZZA

The pizza in Korea stretches the boundaries of what Westerners would call "pizza," and popular chains seem to embrace the more-is-more philosophy. Your pizza will usually have corn on it, and you can have squid, snails, sausage, and chocolate on it, and possibly even all those things together. The biggest pizza chain in Korea is called Mr. Pizza, and it's famous for its stuffed crusts, sweet concoctions, and creative toppings. This pizza recipe is a toned-down version of some popular Korean pizzas, and includes one of the most popular pizza toppings, sweet potato. *Serves 4*

PREP TIME: 30 MINUTES / COOK TIME: 15 MINUTES

Vegetarian-Friendly

1 pound pizza dough or 1 oven-ready pizza crust

1 cup mashed sweet potatoes

2 cups shredded mozzarella cheese, divided

½ green bell pepper, thinly sliced

1 cup stir-fried or grilled Sliced Barbecued Beef (bulgogi, page 178), chopped into small pieces

½ cup thinly sliced mushrooms

2 scallions, chopped, for garnish

Hot red pepper flakes, for serving

INGREDIENT TIP: Koreans loves sweet potatoes. They're eaten as a snack and folded in many other dishes (like pizza). However, the sweet potatoes in Korea are different from the ones you usually find in the United States. They often have speckled purplish skin, have very light flesh (not orange), and are a bit sweeter and nuttier than American sweet potatoes.

1. Preheat the oven to 350°F.

2. If using fresh or frozen pizza dough, roll out to a rectangle or circle that will fit nicely on your baking sheet.

3. Spread a layer of mashed sweet potatoes all over the dough or crust.

4. Sprinkle half of the cheese on top of the sweet potato layer.

5. Distribute the bell peppers, bulgogi meat, and mushrooms over the top of the cheese layer.

6. Finish the pizza by spreading the remaining cheese over the top.

7. Bake for 10 to 15 minutes, or until the crust is browned and the cheese is melted.

8. Garnish with the chopped scallions and serve with hot red pepper flakes on the side.

SUBSTITUTION TIP: For a vegetarian version, omit the bulgogi.

RICE-STUFFED TOFU POCKETS

유부초밥 *yubu chobap*

These tasty little morsels are the Korean version of *inari* sushi, and
they are great for lunchboxes or picnics because you can eat them
hot, cold, or at room temperature. They have premade seasoning
packets for these, which makes it easy, but like other types of sushi,
you can customize it in dozens of different ways. *Serves 4*

PREP TIME: 40 MINUTES / COOK TIME: 0

Vegetarian-Friendly

2 cups cooked white rice

Yubu chobap seasoning package
    (sold with yubu)

⅓ cup steamed sweet corn

⅓ cup steamed sweet peas

6 ounces Canadian bacon or SPAM,
    cut into small dice

1 package yubu (inari, deep-fried tofu pockets)

1. In a large bowl, mix the rice with the
seasoning.

2. Add the corn, peas, and Canadian
bacon (if using).

3. If using SPAM, stir-fry it for 3 to
4 minutes over high heat before adding
it to the rice.

4. Take 2 to 3 tablespoons of the rice
mixture and stuff it gently into each
yubu pocket.

5. Serve immediately, or wrap loosely in
plastic wrap and store in the refrigerator
for up to 3 days.

INGREDIENT TIP: You will find yubu chobap
packages in Asian grocery stores. If
you are using the canned inari pockets,
then soak for 10 minutes and then drain
before using.

INGREDIENT TIP: Yubu Chobap is an easy,
quick meal or snack that's made effort-
less with frozen vegetables. I always try to
have frozen sweet corn, frozen peas, and
frozen broccoli in my freezer for meals
like these.

CURRY RICE

Korean curry rice is a popular dish in homes and casual Korean eateries, but it's very different from Indian curries. The Japanese introduced it to Korea during their occupation, and it was introduced to the Japanese by the British, who had adapted it from traditional Indian curries during the British colonial period. So Korean curry actually tastes very similar to Japanese curry, somewhat similar to British curry, and slightly similar to Indian curries. The easiest and most common way to make Korean curry is to use the prepackaged curry flavor packets; I like the Korean brand Ottogi and the Japanese brand S&B. This is real at-home Korean cooking, and you can make this with beef, chicken, or just vegetables. *Serves 4*

PREP TIME: 20 MINUTES / COOK TIME: 30 MINUTES

Vegetarian-Friendly

1 tablespoon vegetable oil

8 ounces beef, cut into large dice

Salt

Freshly ground black pepper

2 medium potatoes, peeled and
    cut into large dice

1 medium carrot, cut into large dice

2 sweet onions, chopped

3 ounces curry sauce mix
    (this comes in small blocks)

Cooked rice, for serving

Fried eggs, for serving (optional)

SUBSTITUTION TIP: For a vegetarian version, add shiitake mushrooms and vegetable broth instead of the meat and water.

1. Heat the vegetable oil in a deep skillet over medium-high heat. Add the beef and stir-fry for 3 to 4 minutes, adding a dash of salt and pepper.

2. Add the potatoes, carrot, and onions and stir-fry until the vegetables begin to soften, about 5 minutes.

3. Add 3 cups of water to the pot and bring to a boil. Reduce the heat to low and simmer for about 15 minutes.

4. Stir in the curry sauce mix and simmer gently for another 5 minutes. The sauce will continue to thicken even after you remove it from heat.

5. Serve hot, over rice, topped with a fried egg, if desired.

COOKING TIP: You can add a lot of vegetables to this for a more flavorful mix. Try sweet corn, zucchini, and bell peppers.

KIMCHI FRIES
WITH SRIRACHA MAYO

Everyone loves French fries, and this version gives one of the world's most beloved comfort foods a Korean twist. I've included instructions for oven-baked fries for a healthier take on this addictive drinking snack, but you can certainly make it with deep-fried French fries as well. *Serves 6 as a side dish*

PREP TIME: 20 MINUTES / COOK TIME: 35 MINUTES

Vegetarian-Friendly

For the fries

4 Russet potatoes, scrubbed, dried, and cut into matchsticks, and patted dry again

3 tablespoons olive oil

Salt

Freshly ground black pepper

For the kimchi topping

1 cup Napa Cabbage Kimchi (page 54), drained and chopped

2 tablespoons soy sauce

2 tablespoons sugar

½ small sweet onion, chopped

1 tablespoon butter, at room temperature

For the Sriracha mayo

3 tablespoons mayonnaise

1½ tablespoons Sriracha sauce

1 scallion, chopped, for serving

½ cup shredded mozzarella or Cheddar cheese, for serving

TO MAKE THE FRIES

1. Preheat the oven to 450°F.

2. Line two baking sheets with aluminum foil.

3. To make the fries, in a large bowl, toss the potatoes with the olive oil and a few good shakes of salt and pepper.

4. Lay out the potatoes in a single even layer on the prepared baking sheets, dividing them equally.

5. Bake for 30 to 35 minutes, tossing once to ensure even baking.

TO MAKE THE KIMCHI TOPPING

1. While the fries are baking, in a medium bowl, combine the kimchi with the soy sauce, sugar, onion, and butter.

2. Heat a medium skillet over medium heat. Add the kimchi and cook until nicely browned, 4 to 5 minutes.

TO MAKE THE SRIRACHA MAYO

1. In a small bowl, whisk the mayonnaise and Sriracha together.

2. To serve, arrange the fries on a serving dish and top them with the sautéed kimchi.

3. Sprinkle the scallions and cheese over the top, and drizzle with the Sriracha mayo.

VARIATION TIP: You can beef this up with Sliced Barbecued Beef (page 178) or chicken. It's like an umami explosion!

EGG MUFFINS

These savory bites are called "egg bread" in Korea, and they are a convenient, hand-held breakfast. You can make them easily in a muffin tin, and they are perfect for customizing with cheese and fresh herbs. *Makes 8 muffins*

PREP TIME: 10 MINUTES / COOK TIME: 25 MINUTES

Vegetarian-Friendly

1 cup all-purpose white flour

½ teaspoon baking soda

1 teaspoon baking powder

3 tablespoons sugar

½ teaspoon salt

10 eggs

2 tablespoons butter, melted

½ teaspoon vanilla extract

¾ cup milk

Chopped parsley or chives, for garnish (optional)

VARIATION TIP: You can serve these egg muffins with ketchup or hot sauce if you wish. You can also add shredded cheese and thinly sliced cooked bacon to the muffins during the last 10 minutes of cooking time.

1. Preheat the oven to 350°F.

2. Coat the cups of a standard 8-cup muffin tin with cooking spray.

3. In a large bowl, combine the flour, baking soda, baking powder, sugar, and salt.

4. In medium bowl, beat two of the eggs and mix in the butter, vanilla, and milk.

5. Fold the egg mixture into flour mixture and mix until you get a smooth batter.

6. Carefully scoop 1 tablespoon of batter into each muffin cup of the prepared muffin tin.

7. Carefully crack an egg into each muffin cup.

8. Equally distribute the rest of the batter on top of the muffins.

9. Bake for 20 to 25 minutes or until the muffins become golden brown.

10. Serve hot.

CHEESE RAMEN

This will be nothing new if you're Korean or Korean American, but it's wonderful the first time you try it. It elevates prepackaged ramen about a dozen notches on the culinary scale. I don't specify the type of ramen that you should use because I want you to use your favorite type, spicy or not. I like the Sapporo Ichiban brand if I want a nonspicy ramen, and lean toward Shin Ramen if I'm looking for some spice. *Serves 2*

PREP TIME: 3 MINUTES / COOK TIME: 10 MINUTES

Vegetarian-Friendly

1 package instant ramen

¼ sweet onion, thinly sliced

2 eggs

1½ slices American cheese

1. Cook the ramen noodles, along with the onion and the contents of the ramen seasoning packet in a medium saucepan according to the package directions.

2. One minute before the end of the cooking time, crack the eggs into the pot. Pierce each egg yolk with a chopstick, but don't move the eggs around too much.

3. Remove the pot from the heat and add the cheese, stirring gently to met it into the broth.

4. Serve hot.

SUBSTITUTION TIP: If you want to add some meat, then thinly slice 2 slices of Canadian bacon and add it a few minutes before the end of the cooking time.

KOREAN FRIED CHICKEN

닭강정 *dakgangjeong*

Sometimes dubbed "the other KFC," Korean Fried Chicken is twice fried for a super crispy crust and moist meat. It is also usually covered in a super spicy-sweet sauce, but can sometimes be served plain or with other savory sauces. This dish is a popular Korean drinking snack (anju). *Serves 4*

PREP TIME: 15 MINUTES, PLUS 24 HOURS TO MARINATE / COOK TIME: 20 MINUTES

2 pounds chicken drumettes and winglets

1 teaspoon salt

3 tablespoons light brown sugar

1 tablespoon gochujang

2 teaspoons soy sauce

¼ cup soju

2 garlic cloves, grated

¼ small sweet onion, grated

1 teaspoon toasted sesame oil

2 teaspoons gochugaru

Peanut oil for frying

1 tablespoon potato starch or cornstarch

1 teaspoon toasted sesame seeds, for garnish

1. Sprinkle the chicken with salt, cover, and refrigerate for 24 hours.

2. Remove the chicken from the refrigerator and pat dry with paper towels. Put in a large bowl.

3. In a small saucepan, combine the brown sugar, gochujang, soy sauce, soju, garlic, onion, and sesame oil. Bring the mixture to a boil over high heat, and then reduce the heat to low and simmer for about 2 minutes, or until the sauce starts to thicken. Stir in the gochugaru. Strain the sauce through a fine-mesh strainer into a large bowl. Cover and set aside.

4. Add about 2 inches of peanut oil to a heavy-bottomed pot and heat to 320°F, or until the oil starts to bubble, about 5 minutes on high heat.

5. Toss the chicken with the potato starch, coating each piece with a thin layer of starch.

6. Fry the chicken in batches in the hot oil for 8 to 10 minutes, until golden brown. Transfer the chicken wings to a paper towel–lined plate.

7. When all of the chicken has been fried once, fry it a second time for 2 to 3 minutes per batch, adding and heating more oil as needed.

8. Toss the chicken with the sauce in the large bowl.

9. Transfer to a serving platter.and serve garnished with the sesame seeds.

ARMY BASE STEW

부대찌개 *budae chigae*

Budae chigae was invented during the famine years of the Korean War and postwar period. Koreans used leftover food rations handed out from the US Army bases to make this dish (*budae* means military base and *chigae* or *jjigae* means stew in Korean). This is a true fusion dish, born out of necessity, and there is no right way to make it. Budae chigae is usually a lip-smacking mixture of Western meat, ramen noodles, vegetables, and spices. The meat used can be anything and everything including SPAM, hot dogs, ground beef, and sausages; popular vegetable additions are bean sprouts, scallions, onions, and chrysanthemum leaves (*sugkat*). *Serves 4*

PREP TIME: 10 MINUTES / COOK TIME: 30 MINUTES

1½ cups meat in small chunks, like **SPAM, hot dogs, ham, beef, pork, chicken,** or a combination

1½ cups assorted vegetables, like bean sprouts, cabbage, mushrooms, and chrysanthemum leaves

½ yellow onion, sliced

3 tablespoons gochujang

1 package ramen noodles (discard the seasoning packet)

1. In a medium stockpot or saucepan, combine the meat, vegetables, onion, gochujang, and noodles and cover with water. Bring to a rapid boil over high heat. Reduce the heat to low and cook for another 20 minutes.

2. Serve with kimchi and white rice.

VARIATION TIP: Don't be shy about the things you add to this stew. Popular additions include sliced rice cakes, canned baked beans, American cheese, kimchi, and almost anything else you can think of.

KIMCHI HOT DOGS

This is a fun Korean take on the traditional American hot dog, and the gochujang mustard and kimchi relish give it a lot of great spice and flavor. Once you make these condiments, you can use them on other sandwiches too—they're amazing on hamburgers! *Serves 4*

PREP TIME: 10 MINUTES / COOK TIME: 15 MINUTES

2 tablespoons mayonnaise

2 tablespoons yellow mustard

2 tablespoons gochujang

¾ cup Napa Cabbage Kimchi (page 54), drained and chopped

2 teaspoons honey

1 teaspoon soy sauce

½ teaspoon toasted sesame oil

4 beef hot dogs or chicken sausages, lightly scored on the diagonal

4 hot dog buns

1. Preheat the grill to high.

2. To make the gochujang mustard sauce, in a small bowl whisk together the mayonnaise, mustard, and gochujang. Thin with a tiny bit of water if the sauce is too thick. It should be roughly the consistency of ketchup. Set aside.

3. To make the kimchi relish, in another small bowl combine the kimchi with the honey, soy sauce, and sesame oil. Set aside.

4. Grill the hotdogs until nicely browned and crisp. Lightly grill the buns until golden. Put the hot dogs on the buns and top with the kimchi relish, and drizzle with the gochujang mustard sauce.

KIMCHI BULGOGI NACHOS

These Korean fusion nachos are savory, spicy, and simply divine.
There's so much flavor from the bulgogi and the kimchi that this ends
up being more than an appetizer. This might be the perfect drinking snack for gatherings with friends or game nights. *Serves 4*

PREP TIME: 30 MINUTES / COOK TIME: 10 MINUTES

5 cups tortilla chips

1½ cups stir-fried of Sliced Barbecued
    Beef (bulgogi, page 178) or chicken
    bulgogi, cut into bite-size pieces

½ cup shredded mozzarella cheese

½ cup Napa Cabbage Kimchi
    (page 54), drained and sliced

½ cup chunky pico de gallo salsa

¼ cup sliced pickled jalapeño chiles, drained

½ cup Scallion Salad (page 105)

1. Preheat the oven to 350°F.

2. Arrange half the tortilla chips in a
large glass baking dish. Spoon half of the
bulgogi and mozzarella cheese over the
chips. Top with another layer of chips,
meat, and cheese.

3. Bake for 4 to 5 minutes or until the
cheese is nicely melted.

4. To serve, top with the kimchi, salsa,
chiles, and scallion salad.

INGREDIENT TIP: The colors of the kimchi,
cheese, and scallion salad look amazing
against blue corn chips.

Chapter Twelve

DRINKS AND SWEET TREATS

There are not many Korean desserts, and fruit is still probably the most popular after-dinner treat. However, shaved ice (*bingsoo*) is a traditional summertime treat. In this chapter, I've also included some of the traditional Korean sweets eaten and made for special occasions and holidays.

Soju and beer were the most popular Korean alcoholic drinks until very recently, but now cocktails and other types of liquor (including wine) have started to become more popular among Koreans.

SWEET RICE PUNCH

식혜 *sikhye*

This is one of the most traditional Korean after-dinner drinks,
and it often functions as a dessert. It's simple and refreshing,
and is easy to make with an electric rice cooker. *Serves 20*

PREP TIME: 6 HOURS / COOK TIME: 25 MINUTES

Vegan-Friendly, Vegetarian-Friendly

12 ounces barley malt (also called malt powder)

1 gallon water

2 cups cooked rice

1 cup sugar

2 slices fresh peeled ginger

Pine nuts, for garnish (optional)

1. In a very large bowl, mix the malt with the water. Rub the malt with your hands until the liquid becomes cloudy. Strain the liquid through a sieve, and discard the solids.

2. Let the liquid sit for about 2 hours so that the malt settles. You'll be using the clearer liquid on the top.

3. In an electric rice cooker, combine the rice with the clear malt liquid. Turn on the warm setting and let it sit until some rice begins to float, about 4 hours.

4. Transfer the rice with the liquid to a stockpot and add the sugar and ginger. Bring to a boil over high heat and let cook for 15 minutes. Remove from the heat and let cool.

5. Serve cool or cold with a few pine nuts in each cup.

WATERMELON SOJU COCKTAIL

수박소주 *subak soju*

This fun, refreshing cocktail for groups can be served in a pitcher or in a watermelon shell. If you are going for the wow factor, make this with a beautifully symmetrical, bright green watermelon. *Serves 8*

PREP TIME: 15 MINUTES / COOK TIME: 0

Vegetarian-Friendly, Vegan-Friendly

1 medium-size seedless watermelon

1 bottle soju (750 milliliters)

2 cups lemon-lime soda, like Sprite or 7-Up

Juice of ½ lemon

2 cups ice

TIP: For really hot days, make the watermelon soju and store it in a container in the freezer for at least 1 hour. When ready, pour it into the watermelon shell for a refreshing, slushy cocktail.

1. Carefully cut a thin piece of watermelon off the bottom of the watermelon so that it is stable and doesn't wobble. Cut the top off the watermelon, about a quarter of the way down from the top. With a large metal spoon or ladle, scoop out the inside of the watermelon into a large bowl. Use a knife to roughly chop the watermelon flesh in the bowl. Use a potato masher to liquefy most of the watermelon flesh. Remove any fibrous pieces.

2. Add the soju, lemon-lime soda, and lemon juice to the watermelon flesh and stir to mix, continuing to mash and liquefy.

3. When most of the watermelon has broken down, add the watermelon liquid back into the watermelon shell (or into a pitcher if you'd rather pour it).

4. To serve, fill a glass with ice and ladle from the watermelon, or pour the watermelon soju cocktail from the pitcher over the ice.

YOGURT SOJU COCKTAIL

This may sound scary if you've never had a Korean yogurt drink, which is milk-based and watery compared to American yogurt, but it tastes quite good and feels a little healthier than your standard-issue cocktails. This is actually so easy to drink that I would suggest being careful when drinking these. They go down a little bit too easy. *Makes 1 cocktail*

PREP TIME: 5 MINUTES / COOK TIME: 0

Vegetarian-Friendly

1 part soju

1 part Asian yogurt drink

1 part lemon-lime soda, such as Sprite or 7-Up

1. Mix all of the ingredients in a stainless steel shaker full of ice to chill.

2. Pour over ice in a whiskey or highball glass and enjoy.

INGREDIENT TIP: If you don't have access to this Korean yogurt drink, you can make it with American drinkable yogurt and add some milk to it.

GRAPEFRUIT SOJU COCKTAIL

This refreshing cocktail is tart and a little sweet, and it's very easy to make up for brunches, lunches, and summer dinners. *Serves 4*

PREP TIME: 5 MINUTES / COOK TIME: 0

Vegetarian-Friendly, Vegan-Friendly

1½ tablespoons superfine sugar

1 quart grapefruit juice with pulp

1½ cups soju

¼ cup club soda

½ lime, cut into 4 slices, for garnish

1. In a pitcher, stir the sugar into the grapefruit juice until well dissolved. Add the soju and stir to mix.

2. Fill highball glasses with ice and fill each three-quarters full with the grapefruit-soju mixture. Top each glass off with some of the club soda.

3. Garnish with lime slices and serve.

TIP: You can make this with similar proportions with almost any citrus juice, like orange juice or lemonade.

SHAVED ICE WITH SWEET BEANS

팥빙수 *patbingsoo*

This icy cool summer dessert of shaved ice with toppings is one of the most popular Korean hot-weather treats. When I was little, bingsoo was sort of like shaved Italian ice with more toppings, but present-day bingsoo is roughly five times the size of your standard-issue snow cone. Korean cafes create complex shaved ice concoctions, but you can start with this basic *patbingsoo* recipe and feel free to add on at home. If you have a shaved ice machine, then you'll get the perfect consistency of snowy ice to use in your bingsoo. If you don't, you can use a blender or food processor to crush ice cubes into flakes. It won't be exactly the same texture, but it will work. Like most other Korean foods, this is a dish that is meant to be shared. *Serves 3*

PREP TIME: 5 MINUTES / COOK TIME: 5 MINUTES

Vegetarian-Friendly

3 cups shaved ice

¼ cup sweetened condensed milk

¼ cup milk

1 cup sweet red bean paste

1 kiwi, peeled, halved, and sliced

3 strawberries, sliced

½ cup rice cakes, cubed (*injulmi* or *mochi*)

½ banana, sliced

Green tea powder, for garnish

**Scoop of Green Tea Ice Cream
(page 205), for serving (optional)**

1. Put the shaved ice in a serving bowl.

2. Mix the condensed milk and regular milk together in a small bowl and pour over the ice.

3. Top with the bean paste, kiwi, strawberries, rice cakes, banana, and a generous shake of green tea powder.

4. Top with a scoop of green tea ice cream, if desired.

TIP: Have fun with the toppings. Any fruit, whipped cream, cereal, or frozen yogurt work well on bingsoo.

MINT CHOCO BERRY BINGSOO

Although patbingsoo is the original shaved ice dessert, many modern bingsoos don't have any *pat* (red bean) at all. This Mint Choco Berry Bingsoo is a more contemporary recipe, which basically means a gorgeous, huge bowl of frozen goodness. *Serves 3*

PREP TIME: 5 MINUTES / COOK TIME: 5 MINUTES

Vegetarian-Friendly

3 cups shaved ice

¼ cup sweetened condensed milk

¼ cup milk

2 tablespoons Smucker's Chocolate Magic Shell

¼ cup sliced strawberries

¼ cup raspberries

3 tablespoons blueberries

1 large scoop chocolate-mint ice cream

1 tablespoon crushed hazelnuts or pistachios

2 to 3 mint leaves, for garnish

Whipped cream, for serving (optional)

1. Put the shaved ice in a serving bowl.

2. Mix the condensed milk and regular milk together and pour over the ice.

3. Squeeze a generous amount of Chocolate Magic Shell over the shaved ice.

4. Top with the strawberries, raspberries, blueberries, ice cream, and crushed nuts. Garnish with the mint leaves and whipped cream, if desired.

TIP: Chocolate Magic Shell is available in most grocery stores in the dessert aisle near the regular chocolate sauce. Although you can use regular chocolate sauce, Magic Shell hardens when it hits ice cream or ice, so it creates a crackly, crispy layer that adds more texture to your bingsoo.

SESAME CANDIES

깨강정 *kkae gangjeong*

Every Korean kid remembers these sesame cookies (or candies) growing up, but it wasn't until I was an adult that I realized just how easy they are to make. This is the basic recipe for the simple plain black or golden sesame seed squares, but you should feel free to get fancy with different colored sesame seeds and nuts. This recipe is not overly sweet, but you can adjust the sweetness level of the syrup if you find it too sweet or not sweet enough for your taste. *Serves 4*

PREP TIME: 15 MINUTES / COOK TIME: 0

Vegetarian-Friendly

2 cups sesame seeds (golden, black, or a mixture)

1 cup light brown sugar

¾ cup water

¼ cup honey

TIP: You can spice these up with cinnamon, ginger, orange peel, peanuts, and other nuts.

1. In a skillet, toast the sesame seeds over low heat until they start to pop, 4 to 5 minutes. Watch them carefully so they don't burn. Pour the seeds into a plate to cool and set aside.

2. In a medium saucepan over low heat, combine the sugar, water, and honey and stir until the sugar is dissolved. Remove the syrup from heat when it is thick, 5 to 7 minutes.

3. Immediately add the sesame seeds to the syrup, and stir to combine.

4. Line a baking sheet with parchment paper. Spread the sesame seed-syrup mixture evenly onto the pan. Place another piece of parchment paper on top and roll gently with a rolling pin to make sure the top of the candy is flat. Let cool for 5 minutes. Cut with a sharp knife into 1-inch squares or smaller rectangles. (Grease the knife if you have a hard time cutting the candy.)

5. Cool completely and enjoy, or store in an airtight container at room temperature.

GREEN TEA ICE CREAM

Green tea flavors everything from cakes to donuts to ice cream in Korea, and this is an easy and addictive ice cream to make at home. You will need to find natural green tea powder, which you can find in Asian grocery stores and online. The Korean label might be labeled *nokcha karu* and Japanese brands will be called *matcha*. I like a lot of green tea flavor in mine, but you can add more cream and less green tea powder if you'd like a creamier version. *Serves 5*

PREP TIME: 5 MINUTES, PLUS 1 HOUR TO CHILL, PLUS 3 HOURS TO FREEZE / COOK TIME: 20 MINUTES

Vegetarian-Friendly, Gluten-Free

2 to 3 tablespoons green tea powder

⅔ cups sugar

Pinch of sea salt

2 cups half-and-half, warmed for
    15 seconds in the microwave, divided

1. In a small saucepan, whisk together the green tea powder, sugar, salt, and 1 cup of the half-and-half.

2. Heat the mixture slowly over low heat, and slowly stir in the remaining cup of half-and-half.

3. When the mixture is thick enough to coat the back of a spoon and starts to foam, remove it from heat. Let the mixture cool completely.

4. Pour the mixture into a medium bowl, cover, and let chill in refrigerator for at least 1 hour.

5. Churn the mixture for about 20 minutes in an ice cream maker according to the manufacturer's instructions.

6. Transfer to an airtight container and freeze for at least 3 hours before serving.

TIP: For a nondairy version, use full-fat coconut milk instead of the half-and-half.

BROWN SUGAR HOT CAKES

호떡 *hotteok*

These sweet stuffed pancakes are a popular street food and snack in Korea. They are also a popular food for children, and are lovely to eat on a cold winter's day. You can also buy kits for making this in Korean grocery stores. *Serves 8 to 10*

PREP TIME: 30 MINUTES, PLUS 1 HOUR TO RISE / COOK TIME: 50 MINUTES

Vegetarian-Friendly

½ cup warm water

½ tablespoon superfine sugar, plus ½ tablespoon

2 teaspoons dried instant yeast

3 cups sifted all-purpose flour

1 cup milk

½ teaspoon salt

2½ tablespoons light brown sugar

1 teaspoon ground cinnamon

2 tablespoons vegetable oil

1. To make the batter, in a large bowl, combine the water, ½ tablespoon superfine sugar, and yeast. Mix until combined. Set aside for 10 minutes.

2. Add the flour, milk, and salt and mix until a dough begins to form.

3. On a lightly floured work surface, knead the dough for 4 to 5 minutes.

4. Put the dough in the large bowl, cover with plastic wrap, and let it expand and double in size, about 1 hour.

5. To make the filling, in a small bowl, combine the brown sugar, the remaining ½ tablespoon superfine sugar, and cinnamon. Set aside.

6. Dust your hands with flour and roll golf ball–size balls with all the dough.

7. Put one ball in the palm of your hand, flatten with your other hand, and place 1 teaspoon of the filling in the middle. Fold over gently to close. Repeat with the rest of the dough and filling.

8. In batches in a large, lightly oiled skillet over medium-high heat, fry the stuffed dough circles until they puff up, about 2 minutes. Flip and cook until browned, 2 to 3 minutes. Transfer to a paper towel–lined plate. Add more vegetable oil to the pan as needed. Repeat until all of the pancakes have been fried.

9. Serve hot, or enjoy at room temperature.

10. Store in an airtight container at room temperature for up to 2 days.

VARIATION TIP: Experiment with fillings in this one; it's great fun. Try some Nutella or peanut butter!

CANDIED GINGER

편강 *pyeongang*

My grandmother used to make candied citrus peels and candied ginger for the winter. It's so good and easy to make at home. *Serves 8*

PREP TIME: 5 MINUTES / COOK TIME: 1 HOUR

Vegetarian-Friendly,
Vegan-Friendly, Gluten-Free

2 cups thin strips peeled fresh ginger

2 cups granulated sugar, plus more for coating

Brown sugar, for coating

1. In a small stockpot over medium heat, boil the ginger strips gently in water until tender, 20 to 30 minutes. Drain and return the ginger to the pot. Reduce the heat to low.

2. Add the sugar and ¼ cup water, mix to combine, and cook, stirring frequently, until there's almost no liquid left.

3. While the ginger strips are still hot, shake or roll them in granulated sugar and brown sugar. Separate the strips and lay them out on parchment paper to cool.

4. Enjoy this spicy-sweet snack immediately or store in an airtight container up to 2 weeks.

VARIATION TIP: You can slice these candied ginger strips very thin and use them as a garnish for ice cream. You can also use this recipe to make candied orange and lemon peels.

NUT AND RICE CAKES

잡과편 *japgwapyeon*

These sweet dessert rice cakes are made of glutinous rice flour and nuts. Since rice cakes are always given, eaten, or received on holidays or special occasions, you can give these these rice cake balls as a gift or for a special occasion. Although these are very traditional, they are actually remarkably similar to modern-day energy bars or balls, so you can feel free to use them for that purpose if you wish. *Serves 6*

PREP TIME: 10 MINUTES / COOK TIME: 20 MINUTES

Gluten-Free

10 chestnuts, boiled and peeled

2 dried persimmons

4 dates

4 tablespoons pine nuts, diced

1 teaspoon salt

2 cups glutinous rice flour

Honey

INGREDIENT TIP: You can find dried persimmons in Korean and other Asian grocery stores.

1. Dice the chestnuts when they are cool enough to handle. Cut or scrape the seeds out from the dried persimmons and dates. Set the seeds aside. Finely chop the persimmons and dates. In a mortar, pound the seeds with a pestle.

2. In a shallow bowl, mix together the seeds with the chopped persimmons, dates, chestnuts, and pine nuts.

3. In another bowl, add the salt and ¾ cup water to the rice flour and mix until it forms a dough.

4. Add a few more tablespoons of water if it seems too dry.

5. On a clean cutting board, knead dough until it becomes pliable.

6. Roll into 1-inch round balls.

7. In a medium pot, boil the rice balls. When they float, the rice cakes are done.

8. Remove them and rinse them quickly in cold water.

9. Dip the rice cakes in honey and roll them in the mixture of fruit and nuts.

BUCKWHEAT "CAKES"

메밀떡 *memil tteok*

These buckwheat "cakes" are delicious and gluten-free. Like other rice and grain cakes, these were traditionally served and eaten at celebratory or ceremonial events. *Serves 6*

PREP TIME: 10 MINUTES / COOK TIME: 20 MINUTES

Gluten-Free

2 cups buckwheat flour

½ teaspoon sea salt

½ cup water

soybean powder, honey,
    brown sugar (optional)

1. In a bowl, mix together the flour, salt, and water to create a dough. Add a little more water if the dough seems too dry and is unmanageable.

2. On a clean surface, roll out the dough with your hands into ¼-inch-thick rectangles—about six of them.

3. Arrange on a lightly oiled steamer tray. Steam over moderate heat for 10 minutes.

4. Dust or top with soybean powder, honey, and/or brown sugar, if desired.

VARIATION TIP: This is a simple and traditional no-frills recipe, but you can dress these "cakes" up with toppings. I like these with some good honey or brown sugar, but you can also experiment with fruit and preserves. You can also pan-fry these in some oil for a little different texture.

HONEY AND GINGER COOKIES

약과 *yakgwa*

You've probably eaten these before, but they are usually shaped into some sort of flower design if you're buying them. The treat is deep-fried and sweet, so it's more of a dessert than an everyday cookie. The treat was traditionally served at ceremonies, celebrations, and at special occasions.

Yakgwa literally means medicinal confection, since *yak* means medicine and *gwa* means confection or sweet. The medicinal part refers to honey, an important part of Korean traditional medicine. *Makes 20 cookies*

PREP TIME: 40 MINUTES, PLUS 2 TO 3 HOURS FOR SOAKING / COOK TIME: 15 MINUTES

Vegetarian-Friendly

1 cup honey, plus ¼ cup

¼ cup sake

¼ cup water

3 cups all-purpose flour, plus more for dusting

¼ cup toasted sesame oil

½ cup rice malt syrup

1 small piece fresh peeled ginger, thinly sliced

Vegetable oil for frying

¼ cup chopped pine nuts

1 tablespoon toasted sesame seeds

1. In a medium bowl, whisk ¼ cup of the honey, the sake, and water.

2. In a large bowl, mix the flour and sesame oil together with your hands. Rub the flour between your hands and fingers to combine.

3. Add the honey mixture to the flour mixture and knead gently with your hands to form a dough. Wrap in plastic wrap and set aside for 30 minutes.

4. On a lightly floured work surface, roll the dough out until it is ½ inch thick.

5. Cut the dough into 1-inch strips and shape into rectangles. Make a small hole in the center of each cookie.

6. In a small saucepan, mix together the rice malt syrup, the remaining 1 cup honey, and ginger and heat over medium heat. Bring to a simmer and remove the pan immediately from the heat. Pour the syrup into a rectangular glass baking dish. Set aside.

7. Fill a sturdy, flat-bottomed fryer, wok, or skillet one-third full with vegetable oil. Heat over medium heat until the oil temperature is 212°F on a candy thermometer.

8. In small batches, drop the pastries into the oil and fry, gently turning them, until they puff and float, about 4 minutes. Raise the heat of the oil to about 300°F and continue to fry until the pastries turns a golden brown. Transfer to the baking dish with the ginger syrup. Turn each one over to coat with syrup. Repeat, until all the pastries are cooked.

9. Let the cookies soak in the syrup for 2 to 3 hours, and then remove them with a slotted spoon to a parchment-lined baking dish to drain.

10. Sprinkle with pine nuts and sesame seeds.

11. Store at room temperature in an airtight containter for up to 1 week.

VARIATION TIP: If I make these at home, I shape them into rectangles. But you can shape them into whatever shape you wish, like circles or twists.

ACKNOWLEDGMENTS

There are so many people who made this book possible, including many talented people at Rockridge Press. I want to thank my editor, Clara Song Lee, whose vision made this all happen, and who really sold me on the idea for this book. I'm also thankful to Robin Donovan, the development editor who kept me on task, and to Ellen Wheat, the copy editor who polished everything with her meticulous eye.

I am thankful to my family and friends, and for my sons and husband who go through all the highs and lows of recipe testing with me.

TIPS FOR DINING OUT

Dining out in Korea or in a Korean restaurant is a unique experience if it's new to you. Here's a brief guide to get you through, although some of these things will not be true at Western or at fancy restaurants in Korea, and in more Americanized Korean restaurants in America.

Restaurants in Korea are very specialized and are known for a specific type of food or even only a few dishes. This is also true of many Korean restaurants in Koreatown in Los Angeles, New York City, and the Washington, DC, metro area.

COURSES AND SIDE DISHES

The first thing you'll notice is that Korean meals are not served in courses. So as soon as you order, your server will bring you an array of side dishes. These come with your meal and are usually unlimited. You can eat these as appetizers if you're hungry, but they are really side dishes to your full meal.

WAITERS AND SERVICE

If you need to call your server, look for a button on the table. If there is one, press it and your server will come to you. It's very similar to the call button that you'd use in

an airplane. If there's no button, then it's okay to call out to your server.

SHARING DISHES

Korean food is all about sharing, and that means that people do traditionally double dip into side dishes. People try to be conscious of only picking up and touching what they'll eat, but if you are uncomfortable with this custom, put a little bit of each side dish on an extra plate for yourself.

DRINKS

Koreans usually don't drink water with their meals. Barley tea is one of the most popular drinks served at a Korean restaurant, because it is supposed to help with digestion. You can drink this warm, hot, or cold. Feel free to ask for ice water if you want it. When drinking alcohol, do try to follow the traditional Korean drinking etiquette if you're dining with Korean nationals (see "Eat, Drink, and Be Merry," page 24). Beer and soju are also commonly consumed during dinner.

CONVERSION TABLES

VOLUME EQUIVALENTS (LIQUID)

US STANDARD	US STANDARD (OUNCES)	METRIC (APPROXIMATE)
2 tablespoons	1 fl. oz.	30 mL
¼ cup	2 fl. oz.	60 mL
½ cup	4 fl. oz.	120 mL
1 cup	8 fl. oz.	240 mL
1½ cups	12 fl. oz.	355 mL
2 cups or 1 pint	16 fl. oz.	475 mL
4 cups or 1 quart	32 fl. oz.	1 L
1 gallon	128 fl. oz.	4 L

OVEN TEMPERATURES

FAHRENHEIT (F)	CELSIUS (C) (APPROXIMATE)
250°	120°
300°	150°
325°	165°
350°	180°
375°	190°
400°	200°
425°	220°
450°	230°

VOLUME EQUIVALENTS (DRY)

US STANDARD	METRIC (APPROXIMATE)
⅛ teaspoon	0.5 mL
¼ teaspoon	1 mL
½ teaspoon	2 mL
¾ teaspoon	4 mL
1 teaspoon	5 mL
1 tablespoon	15 mL
¼ cup	59 mL
⅓ cup	79 mL
½ cup	118 mL
⅔ cup	156 mL
¾ cup	177 mL
1 cup	235 mL
2 cups or 1 pint	475 mL
3 cups	700 mL
4 cups or 1 quart	1 L

WEIGHT EQUIVALENTS

US STANDARD	METRIC (APPROXIMATE)
½ ounce	15 g
1 ounce	30 g
2 ounces	60 g
4 ounces	115 g
8 ounces	225 g
12 ounces	340 g
16 ounces or 1 pound	455 g

THE DIRTY DOZEN
AND THE CLEAN FIFTEEN

A nonprofit and environmental watchdog organization called Environmental Working Group (EWG) looks at data supplied by the US Department of Agriculture (USDA) and the Food and Drug Administration (FDA) about pesticide residues and compiles a list each year of the best and worst pesticide loads found in commercial crops. You can refer to the Dirty Dozen list to know which fruits and vegetables you should always buy organic. The Clean Fifteen list lets you know which produce is considered safe enough when grown conventionally to allow you to skip the organics. This does not mean that the Clean Fifteen produce is pesticide-free, though, so wash these fruits and vegetables thoroughly.

These lists change every year, so make sure you look up the most recent before you fill your shopping cart. You'll find the most recent lists as well as a guide to pesticides in produce at EWG.org/FoodNews.

2015 DIRTY DOZEN

Apples	In addition to the
Celery	Dirty Dozen, the
Cherry tomatoes	EWG added two foods contaminated
Cucumbers	with highly toxic
Grapes	organo-phosphate
Nectarines	insecticides:
Peaches	Hot peppers
Potatoes	Kale/Collard greens
Snap peas	
Spinach	
Strawberries	
Sweet bell peppers	

2015 CLEAN FIFTEEN

Asparagus	Mangoes
Avocados	Onions
Cabbage	Papayas
Cantaloupe	Pineapples
Cauliflower	Sweet corn
Eggplant	Sweet peas (frozen)
Grapefruit	Sweet potatoes
Kiwis	

RESOURCES

The Internet has made the world a lot smaller, and this is a great thing if you're looking for a hard-to-find spice or ingredient or the best places to eat in Seoul or in Koreatown in New York.

RECOMMENDED WEBSITES FOR PURCHASING KOREAN FOOD

H-Mart *hmart.com*

H-Mart has brick-and-mortar stores and online shopping, and they have a good selection of prepared foods, packaged foods, and housewares.

Koa Mart *kaomart.com*

This website mostly has nonperishables, but they also have an excellent selection of condiments and packaged foods.

Amazon *amazon.com*

This online megastore sells everything these days, including kimchi, prepared foods, and Korean spices and condiments.

KOREAN AND ASIAN MARKETS

There are a few big chains with locations in the New York City and Los Angeles metro areas. Check their websites to see if they have a store near you.

H-Mart *hmart.com*

Han Kook Market
hankooksupermarket.com

Han Nam *hannamchain.com*

If you don't live near a Korean market but you are close to a Chinatown, then that's a great place to go for some of the harder-to-find fresh ingredients. You can buy your Korean spices and condiments online (there will be more variety to choose from), but you'll have better luck getting vegetables in Chinatown. You can stock up on daikon and other Asian radishes, different types of Asian greens, napa cabbage, and a huge variety of mushrooms, including king oyster and enoki. You'll also probably be able to find dried anchovies, roots, and other specialty ingredients.

OTHER ONLINE RESOURCES

For more recipes and information about Korean food, visit some of these websites.

RECIPES, TUTORIALS, AND COOKING VIDEOS

aeriskitchen.com
koreanfood.about.com
maangchi.com

FOOD SCENE IN KOREA, KOREAN FOOD CULTURE

zenkimchi.com
seouleats.com

INDEX

CPSIA information can be obtained
at www.ICGtesting.com
Printed in the USA
BVHW020806080819
555304BV00040B/378/P